Sexual Trauma among Girls in Educational Settings

This book uses an intersectional lens to explore the lived experiences of sexually traumatized girls in school. It provides a deep understanding of the students' experiences, viewed through the prism of their multiple identities. The author employs a qualitative phenomenological study to investigate the psychological, social, and academic impacts of such trauma.

The book's core strength lies in its exploration of the intersectionality between identity and sexual trauma. It does this by examining the impacts of historical trauma, through the lens of four major historical events: transatlantic slavery, the Holocaust, World War II, and the COVID-19 pandemic. This research highlights potential mental health, social, and academic outcomes prevalent in historically marginalized groups, which is then connected to a broader understanding of intersectionality and trauma. It underscores the urgent need for educators and school leaders to understand this phenomenon in order to be effective in their roles. The book also emphasizes the importance of addressing trauma in educational settings, considering the intersectionality of identity, trauma, and educational experience. The book also proposes an additional identity marker to support Crenshaw's theory of intersectionality: female sexual trauma survivor.

This book is a valuable resource for scholars, educators, educational leaders, post-graduate students, and policymakers. It offers research-based theoretical approaches to addressing trauma and intersectionality in educational contexts. It is a must-read for those seeking to broaden their understanding of these complex issues and their impact on educational experiences for female sexual trauma survivors.

Jennifer Etesse Herring is Adjunct Professor at the Lesley Institute for Trauma Sensitivity (LIFTS), Lesley University, USA, and the founder of Herring Hope and Healing, a trauma consulting and coaching business that coaches sexual trauma survivors and their families.

Routledge Research in Education

This series aims to present the latest research from right across the field of education. It is not confined to any particular area or school of thought and seeks to provide coverage of a broad range of topics, theories, and issues from around the world.

On the Theory of Content Transformation in Education
The 3A Methodology for Analysing and Improving Teaching and Learning
Tomáš Janík, Jan Slavík, Petr Najvar and Tereza Češková

Living Educational Theory Research as an Epistemology for Practice
The Role of Values in Practitioners' Professional Development
Jack Whitehead and Marie Huxtable

Empowering Teachers for Equitable and Sustainable Education
Action Research, Teacher Agency, and Online Community
Maria Teresa Tatto

Theory and Practice of STEAM Education in Japan
Edited by Tetsuo Isozaki

Engaging Critical Pedagogy in Education
Global Phenomenon, Local Praxis
Edited by Fida Sanjakdar and Michael W. Apple

International Perspectives on Educational Administration using Educational Inquiry
Conceptual and Theoretical Approaches
Edited by Abdulrasheed Olowoselu and Areej ElSayary

For more information about this series, please visit: www.routledge.com/Routledge-Research-in-Education/book-series/SE0393

Sexual Trauma among Girls in Educational Settings

Intersectional Identities and Trauma-Informed Care

Jennifer Etesse Herring

NEW YORK AND LONDON

First published 2025
by Routledge
605 Third Avenue, New York, NY 10158

and by Routledge
4 Park Square, Milton Park, Abingdon, Oxon, OX14 4RN

Routledge is an imprint of the Taylor & Francis Group, an informa business

ISBN: 978-1-032-64864-4 (hbk)
ISBN: 978-1-032-64865-1 (pbk)
ISBN: 978-1-032-64866-8 (ebk)

DOI: 10.4324/9781032648668

Typeset in Times New Roman
by KnowledgeWorks Global Ltd.

Contents

Introduction

This book is written to discuss the school experiences of women who have experienced sexual trauma. The text is based on my research study conducted in fulfillment of my doctoral research. The study was phenomenological and was anchored in survivor stories through the lens of intersectionality theory. The original and more recent definitions of intersectionality are discussed as well as proposing an additional marker of identity, "sexual trauma survivor" as reported by study participants who for the purposes of this book are known as "survivors." This book takes the reader on a journey through the reported lived experiences of survivors in school settings to highlight the three findings of the study and provide opportunities for educators and school leaders to shift current professional practices that have shifted infrequently since the birth of public education—current educational practices are especially ineffective for students who are typically at high risk for and/or are survivors of sexual trauma.

Survivors (participants) of the study were adult women who consented to participate to recall and report their childhood school experiences through a series of interview questions that sought to understand positive and negative experiences in school post-trauma. The findings of the study emerged out of themes that were identified based on patterns and repetition in individual survivor interviews. While this book seeks to reach a wide audience, it specifically seeks to primarily engage the students who will benefit from this research whether from personal lived experiences of that of a peer or relative.

The book contains eight chapters, which discuss the introduction to the text, a literature review and methodology chapter, one chapter for each of the findings of the study, strategies and recommendations and conclusions.

Many of my personal and professional experiences have informed my thinking and interest in improving school support available to students who have survived sexual trauma. As a domestic violence advocate, educator and current urban school administrator, I have been able to take a critical look at how the needs of sexually traumatized girls are understood and addressed in schools. Based on what I have observed in schools and classrooms, and what current data show about sexual trauma survivors, I have become increasingly

DOI: 10.4324/9781032648668-1

interested in learning what sexually traumatized girls need to enhance their social and academic growth in school.

The rationale for conducting a qualitative phenomenological study is that it is exploratory and open-ended, not confirmatory. Secondly, there is currently not enough research on the populations of women represented in this study. Additionally, there is a complexity of trauma, which leads to the necessity of incorporating multiple perspectives of the phenomenon. Next, not only is there an underrepresentation of historically marginalized communities and their experiences in the literature, but there is a lack on studies that examine outcomes for the populations using studies that may inform educational practices such as studies that link the impact of sexual trauma on mental health, physical health and culture or the impact of perceptions of sexual trauma survivors of color in the implementation of law and public policy. Last, the use of intersectionality as a framework to understand the complexity of sexual trauma survival because it draws the reader's attention to the multiple identities of a survivor and how the identities interact with larger systems. For the purposes of this book, the system that will be examined in relation to identities is the United States Educational System.

Because of the complexity of sexual trauma, it is important to note that this book does not recommend educators or school support staff to guide, coerce or influence sexual trauma disclosure from students or caregivers. There are also no specific clinical or legal recommendations for school-related interventions for or on behalf of student survivors. This book seeks to provide multiple first-hand lived experiences of sexual trauma survivors to encourage a more broad conversation that creates a sense of urgency to think more systematically about what general shifts in educational practice need to be made in order to promote systemic change in educational settings that would not only benefit students who have experienced sexual trauma, but ultimately benefit all students.

I have designed the study to answer three guiding questions of how educators can effectively support female survivors of sexual trauma in school by anchoring the first steps to solution-seeking in the lived experiences of sexual trauma survivors. This book argues that the impact of sexual trauma is intersectional in nature and is not currently being mitigated effectively in general educational settings. The goal of this book is to provide a research-based understanding of the impact of sexual trauma on girls through the lens of intersectionality.

Why This Book?

The purpose of this study is to gain a deeper understanding of the school experiences of sexual trauma survivors and how to effectively support them using a lens of intersectionality in school systems. This study explores the school experiences of girls who have survived sexual trauma and the nuance that exists in each individual and in female sexual trauma survivors as a collective community. Because there is limited literature that specifically addresses the educational and social needs of girls who have experienced trauma when in school (Blodgett & Dorado, 2016), this study documents the language that captures the lived experiences of women who have a history of sexual trauma. I wanted to learn what female survivors of sexual trauma recalled and reported about their school experiences after their traumatizing event(s). Additionally, I was interested in understanding what, if any, programs, people, and aspects of the school environment helped mitigate the impact of sexual trauma. Last, I was curious about what conditions, if any, helped foster academic and social achievement and growth as well as satisfaction in school. The purpose of this study was not to discuss the traumatic event(s) experienced by survivors.

The goal of the study was to learn from the survivors themselves what their school experiences were in light of their identity as a sexual trauma survivor and to provoke conversation about how educational systems may begin to shift overall practices in the field of education for the purpose of building systems that are meant to support students who have experienced sexual trauma. The study is Based on a phenomenological nature of the study, and it brings attention to what survivors reported that they needed as students during their time in school. The study gives insight to educators and additional school personnel who are curious about how to strengthen their current practice to be more inclusive of sexual trauma survivors in schools.

Readers of this book will have access to a representative account of the voices of female childhood sexual trauma survivors. The study will serve as a beginning point of conversation between all key stakeholders on how to rethink general current practices in the field of education. The study connects to the guiding research questions by opening up an opportunity for women to share their lived experiences of navigating school, given their history of sexual trauma. The ultimate hope was to create a safe space for participants to report their authentic lived experiences in school as sexual trauma survivors to communicate recommendations that can be a catalyst for shifting general educational practices. The findings of the study emerged from the themes that appeared in survivor responses. Survivor responses were analyzed for the identification of trends and patterns as well as an overall understanding of female sexual trauma survivor school experiences post-trauma. I seek to answer the question: *What can educators and educational leaders do to better support female sexual trauma survivors in school?*

The book shares fourteen survivor stories of navigating educational systems post-trauma. Each of the findings chapters starts with first-hand accounts of survivor statements that honor the lived experiences of each, while also framed as a single survivor story to help magnify and humanize sexual trauma survival of girls.

Survivor stories are shared to highlight the multi-faceted challenges that come up as a result of sexual trauma. These stories help guide the reader to humanize the experience of sexual trauma survival in school. These stories also reflect the current state of the literature regarding supporting sexual trauma in schools.

1 Theoretical and Conceptual Framework

This chapter seeks to guide the reader through the understanding of what it is like to walk in the shoes of female sexual trauma survivors in school. The conversation starts with attending to the voices of sexual trauma survivors that might be otherwise hidden. The purpose of this approach is to understand where the opportunities are for shifting practice in schools to create environments that are safe for female survivors of sexual trauma to learn. To answer the question: *What can schools do to support girls who have experienced childhood sexual trauma?* First, while according to the literature, prevalence of sexual abuse of girls is high, it is even higher among girls who are part of historically marginalized populations. The three experiences that will be examined in this chapter are: being a female sexual trauma survivor, intersectional identity experiences, and school experiences.

These three experiences within each individual survivor story will help illuminate for readers the educational needs and opportunities for female survivors in school. Additionally, the three experiences discussed are how I define the "complexity" of sexual trauma. There must be an understanding of how the complex nature of sexual trauma can exacerbate the school experience of female sexual trauma survivors.

According to research, schools are currently not equipped to support the needs of girls who have experienced sexual trauma. Current understandings of sexual trauma of school-aged girls are fragmented (Chamberlain et al., 2006; Jones & McNally, 2022; Miragoli et al., 2017). Today, research on trauma is limited to the psychological and biological impacts of general trauma, with even less available information on the impact of sexual trauma on girls of color (Blodgett & Dorado, 2016). I found it necessary to extract from existing research from both general trauma and sexual trauma researchers where applicable to show the contrast of available literature in each domain. Some of the prominent trauma research I reference dates back to the 1990s (Mambrol, 2018). In doing this, I am able to capture the most recent research that has been done about general trauma, while centering the attention needed on sexual trauma and how it impacts learning and the

DOI: 10.4324/9781032648668-2

school experience. The examination of the two areas of research will help draw the reader's attention to the need for understanding how schools can shift practice to more effectively support girls who have experienced sexual trauma.

A 2003 national survey of adolescents shows an overwhelming prevalence of sexual assault, physical assault, physically abusive punishment, and witnessing acts of violence. Rates of victimization among 12–17-year-olds are high, yet estimates suggest that 86% of sexual assaults and 65% of physical assaults went unreported. A clear relationship was also found between victimization, mental health problems, and delinquency, with findings specific to gender, race, and ethnicity. More than half of Black, Hispanic, and Native American adolescents had witnessed violence in their lifetimes. In each group, 20–25% reported experiencing sexual assault. Over 30% of these assaults happened in the victim's home (Kilpatrick et al., 2003).

There is much written about the impact that sexual trauma has on brain development and its subsequent effect on how individuals participate in an academic environment. According to research, trauma impacts development, behavior, learning, and social connections (Cole et al., 2005). Adverse traumatic experiences like sexual violations inhibit close relational ties that are critical for brain development. Providing an environment in which children can experience healthy connections, reorganize relationships through sensory and interpersonal experiences, and thereby providing an environment that facilitates this brain-repair process (Banks, 2006; Blodgett & Dorado, 2016; Krüger & Fletcher, 2017). In addition, DeBellis et al. (2009) found that psychobiological research on trauma is inherently complex because of the likelihood that children suffering from different subtypes of neglect often have other psychobiological and psychosocial compromises and outcomes.

Scholars have shared how schools respond to trauma and how informed schools have created an environment that makes it feasible for students who have experienced trauma to navigate school and build resiliency. Although girls may not always self-disclose, if they have experienced sexual assault, they do often exhibit behaviors that may appear to be oppositional or defiant. There is an interplay between school culture and discipline. Therefore, there is a close relationship between how teachers generally perceive their students and how they carry out consequences for misbehavior (Cole et al., 2005). The hope readers of this book will gain a deeper understanding of the school experiences of female sexual trauma survivors and potential changes in general educational practices overall. This study documented the words of women who have a history of sexual trauma and their recollections of their school experiences as girls. Last, I was curious about what conditions, if any, helped foster sexual trauma survivor success and satisfaction in school.

Guiding Research Questions

The following research questions guide this qualitative study:

RQ1: *What do sexual trauma survivors recall about their academic and social middle and high school experiences?*

RQ2: *What systems, factors, and conditions, if any, do survivors report as most supportive in middle and high school?*

RQ3: *What do survivors of sexual trauma want educators to know based on their lived experiences?*

In an attempt to be mindful of what discussing childhood memories could trigger for participants, I assumed that asking questions about middle and high school were safe times of development to discuss. However, while questions asked were geared toward middle and high school, all participants in this study found that reflecting back as far as Kindergarten more accurately shaped their school experience following their sexually traumatizing event(s).

Who Can Benefit from This Book?

In the literature about trauma-sensitive practices in schools, it is suggested that educators be trained on how to provide a supportive learning environment for students who have experienced trauma (Blodgett & Dorado, 2016; Cole et al., 2005). The study was phenomenological by nature. The rationale of the methodology for the study was to understand first-hand accounts of survivor school experiences post-trauma. The study allowed me to utilize survivors' stories to see if their school experiences were positive or negative. I also sought to understand if survivor experiences were a result of their schools adopting trauma-sensitive approaches to teaching and learning in school. Survivors chose to participate in the study based on their comfort level with discussing their school experiences post-trauma. The coding of themes of participant stories was based on patterns and trends in participant responses – particularly responses having to do with the intersections of identity, trauma, and school experiences post-trauma.

Because schools have not yet understood how to best respond to the needs of survivors of sexual trauma, the accounts collected in this study were instructive. The systems, conditions, and programs that participants describe as supportive will help design more trauma-sensitive schools in the future. The recommendations these survivors share will provide needed insights for girls in school who have experienced sexual trauma, their educators, school leaders, and their families.

Because the literature (Blodgett & Dorado, 2016; Chafouleas et al., 2016; Gresham, 2007), it is clear that no one approach to trauma can be applied to all survivors (as each person has a different reaction to their trauma). This book will impact sexual trauma survivors, educators, school leaders, caregivers, advocates, and anyone who has influence in developing educational policies on behalf of girls who have experienced sexual trauma.

Although the study focuses on girls who have experienced sexual trauma, male survivors can benefit from this study because the honesty with which survivors share can help all students who are enduring sexual trauma obtain success in school. While trauma impacts each individual differently, male survivors can most certainly find similarities or areas where they can relate to the reflections of the survivor reports in this study.

Educators can benefit from this book because of the growing body of research about instructional strategies and best practices in addressing trauma in schools. While schools that are aware of the challenge of trauma tend to focus on general trauma, this study can provide specialized knowledge about the needs of girls who have experienced sexual trauma.

Parents and caregivers of survivors will benefit from this study because they will have multiple examples of how girls have navigated the academic and social demands of school while surviving trauma during their school years. Because sexual trauma is complex by nature, the stories of survivors are complex as well. This is beneficial because the complexity increases the likelihood that girls who have survived sexual trauma find experiences that they can relate to and begin steps toward academic and social success.

Definition of Terms

Because of the considerable scope of the problem of trauma, it is necessary to define key terms in the context of this research.

Complex PTSD. The current understanding of the multi-faceted impact of trauma on the human brain, body, and emotions across all developmental stages (Figley et al., 2017).

Educational Experience. All academic and social aspects of time in school (Gutek, 1995).

Historical Trauma. Historical trauma examines historical challenges of cultural groups spanning but not limited to challenges concerning health, biology, pregnancy and birth, child-rearing, emotional and mental health, and financial stability (Sotero, 2006).

Intersectionality Theory. This theory emphasizes the crossing and tension between multiple identities and experiences that inform the self-concept of a woman (Crenshaw, 1989).

Racism. Systemic oppression that is created to perpetuate lack of access for historically marginalized populations. Access to resources includes but is not limited to healthcare, education, equal pay for equal or more work, physical environment, and upward mobility (Crenshaw, 1989; Walby et al., 2012).

Resilience. The ability to produce positive academic and health outcomes despite trauma (Ledesma, 2014).

Retraumatization. Retraumatization is defined as intentionally or unintentionally creating conditions in a space that cause one or more individuals or groups in the space to be reminded by their traumatic experience(s) (SAMHSA, 2014; Zgoda et al., 2020).

Sexual Assault. Any bodily harm done of a sexual nature including but not limited to rape, molestation, exploitation/prostitution, fondling, or forced oral sex. Cook et al. (2003) of the National Child Traumatic Stress Network Complex Trauma Task Force describe more diagnostic criteria for sexual trauma – lack of behavior regulation, under-controlled or over-controlled behavior patterns, and impaired cognitive functioning.

Sexual Trauma. The response to an adverse experience often leading to developmental and cognitive delays that result from the trauma of sexual assault. Herman (1992) defines trauma as both a psychological event and a relational event. Trauma is multi-faceted because it has various effects on the survivor.

Survivors. Females who have experienced some form of sexual assault.

Trauma. Herman (1992), a pioneer in the field of trauma, defines trauma as a result of a psychological event and a relational event. Signs include: withdrawal, aggression, delinquent behavior, and sexualized behavior are common in sexual abuse survivors (Brown & Finkelhor, 1992). Symptoms include: distrust of authority figures, aggression, hypervigilance, and seeking alliances with the most violent person in any situation are common life beliefs and patterns seen in children who have been traumatized (Burgess et al., 1998).

The study in this book is grounded in the research of Crenshaw (1989)'s intersectionality theory. This theory allowed me to anchor this work in understanding the significance of identity as it impacts learning in schools. Intersectionality theory addresses the challenges that women of color face in societal systems. Despite its current controversy (Solorzano et al., 2000), Crenshaw uses intersectionality to address larger systemic challenges that often have to do with engaging with the stories and testimonies of women who hold multiple identities to drive systemic change.

The highlighting of "women of color" based on the research does not negate the impact of sexual trauma on White girls but rather is an attempt to grow research that intentionally focuses on outcomes that emerge from the sexual trauma of those who historically and currently have been under-researched and under-supported. While research suggests that sexual trauma impacts women of color more, I acknowledge how sexual trauma impacts White girls just as severely. I also act on this personal belief in this book by referring to survivors of sexual trauma as being part of "historically marginalized communities" rather than only "girls of color." This framing is important to me because it recognizes that White girls can also be part of historically marginalized communities (class, economics, immigration status, etc) even if the only identity marker is "sexual trauma survivor." As such, I choose to center my research on uniting the experience of female sexual trauma survivors across all identity markers rather than centering the experience based on race.

Despite my personal belief on the framing of this issue, the academic research that I reference and lean on emphasizes "girls of color" as the most vulnerable. Throughout this book, I will offer opportunities to frame this as a challenge for "historically marginalized communities" and offer ways to reimagine education that will benefit all female survivors of sexual trauma and survivors of trauma in general. Over time, the research and examination of the theory of intersectionality became broader to any and all individuals who identify as part of a historically marginalized group. Current research on intersectionality extends interdisciplinarity and helps to inform creating a basis of knowledge and understanding of how the lived experiences of individuals and communities of historically marginalized identities impact the space they occupy (Coaston, 2019).

One of the themes that emerged out of the research study was that survivors of the study reported their experience of sexual trauma as ingrained as part of their identity as much as their race or ethnicity. This was even more true for survivors whose abuse began at an early age. This reality for survivors brought to light for me the depth of knowledge survivors have on how sexual trauma impacts identity.

While I am in no way stating that to be a sexual trauma survivor is to be an advocate for policy change for all survivors, I am curious about the systems that currently exist in education and whether or not the identities that have been historically marginalized feel safe and supported in influencing change in educational practices that can have a lasting impact for all survivors of sexual trauma in school. Or, do the identity markers of sexual trauma survivors default into a more silent supporter or full invisibilizing of the self because of taboo and who is typically centered when considering creating systemic change?

In January 2023, the United States Department of Health & Human Services discussed the value of using lived experiences to inform and shape research and policy. There are current needs recognized and acknowledged by The Department of Health and Human Services (HHS) to ensure that policies are implemented based on the lived experiences reported. According to the Department of Health and Human Services, it is necessary to engage in the work of meeting community needs based on lived experience through the lens of equity. In the list of equitable approaches to engaging lived experiences to shape policy, the following are noted:

- It is important to hold time and space for authentic connection with individuals with lived experiences and policymakers to bridge gaps and facilitate internalization of lived experiences.
- Safe and honest spaces and conversations must be prioritized in order to be able to capture the most authentic positioning of individuals sharing their lived experiences and making an impact.
- Inclusive and sensitive language must be used to provide a sense of safety and belonging in the space and highlight the assets of the individuals sharing their lived experience from an asset lens rather than a deficit mindset.
- Respect must be demonstrated to participants as well as respect for their stories.
- Expect discomfort.
- There must be sensitivity to the values that people hold.
- Recognize and acknowledge structural bias that impacts individual lived experiences.
- Engage people in the decision-making process (HHS, 2023).

The methodology of the study addresses all areas of focus of the Department of Health and Human Services. As the lead researcher in this study, I had to ensure that survivors felt safe enough to share their school experiences as well as add additional perspectives on how their trauma has impacted them as students. Measures were taken to ensure minimal risk of harm to all study participants. The focus on safety, honoring values, and understanding how systemic bias impacts people speaks directly to the study being conducted through the lens of intersectionality. The goal of this book is for the reader to consider new ways to approach systems of education based on the stories shared by survivors of sexual trauma in the study.

References

GUTECK, DHHS, van der Kolk 2003, Zgoda

Banks, A. (2006). Relational therapy for trauma. *Journal of Psychological Trauma, 5*(1), 25–47. https://doi.org/10.1300/J189v05n01_03

Blodgett, C. (2012). Adopting ACEs Screening and Assessment in Child Serving Systems.

Blodgett, C. (2014). ACEs in Head Start Children and Impact on Development.

Blodgett, C., & Dorado, J. (2016). A Selected Review of Trauma-Informed School Practice and Alignment with Educational Practice. http://ext100.wsu.edu/cafru/wpcontent/uploads/sites/65/2015/02/CLEAR-Trauma-Informed-Schools-White-Paper.pdf

Browne A. & Finkelhor D. (1992). *Impact* https://10.1037//0033-2909.99.1.66

Burgess, A., Groth, N., Holmstrom, L., & Srgoi, S. (1998). *The sexual assault of children and adolescents*. Lexington Books.

Chafouleas, S.M., Johnson, J.H., Overstreet, S., & Santos, N.M., (2016). Toward a blueprint for trauma-informed service delivery in schools. *School Mental Health, 8*: 144–162.

Chamberlain, P., Leve, L. D., & Smith, D. K. (2006). Preventing behavior problems and health risking behaviors. *International Journal of Behavioral Consultation and Therapy, 2*(4). http://files.eric.ed.gov/fulltext/EJ804058.pdf

Cole, S. F., O'Brien, J. G., Gadd, M. G., Ristuccia, J., Wallace, D. L., & Gregory, M. (2005). *Helping traumatized children learn: Supportive school environments for children traumatized by family violence*. Massachusetts Advocates for Children.

Cook, A., Blaustein, M., Spinazzola, J., & van der Kolk, B. (Eds.) (2003). *Complex trauma in children and adolescents*. National Child Traumatic Stress Network. http://www.NCTSNet.org

Crenshaw, K. (1989) "Demarginalizing the Intersection of Race and Sex: A Black Feminist Critique of Antidiscrimination Doctrine, Feminist Theory and Antiracist Politics," *University of Chicago Legal Forum*: Vol. 1989, Article 8. https://chicagounbound.uchicago.edu/uclf/vol1989/iss1/8

DeBellis, M. D., Hooper, S. R., Spratt, E. G., & Woolley, D. P. (2009). Neuropsychological findings in childhood neglect and their relationships to pediatric PTSD. *Journal of International of Neuropsychological Society, 15*(6), 869–878.

Figley, C. R., Ellis, A. E., Reuther, B. T., & Gold, S. N. (2017). The study of trauma: A historical overview. In S. N. Gold (Ed.), *APA handbook of trauma psychology: Foundations in knowledge* (pp. 1–11). American Psychological Association. https://doi.org/10.1037/0000019-001

Gresham, F. M. (2007). Evolution of the response-to-intervention concept: Empirical foundations and recent developments. In S. R. Jimerson, M. K. Burns, & A. VanDerHayden (Eds.), *Handbook of Response to Intervention: The science and practice of assessment and intervention* (pp. 10–24). Springer.

Gutek BA, Koss MP (1993), Changed women and changed organizations: consequences of and coping with sexual harassment. *J Vocat Behav 42*(1):28–48.

Herman, J. (1992). Complex PTSD: A syndrome in survivors of prolonged and repeated trauma. *Journal of Traumatic Stress. 5*(3). http://66.199.228.237/boundary/Childhood_trauma_and_PTSD/complex_PTSD.pdf

Jones, P. J., & McNally, R. J. (2022). Does broadening one's concept of trauma undermine resilience? *Psychological Trauma: Theory, Research, Practice, and Policy, 14*(S1), S131–S139. https://doi.org/10.1037/tra0001063

Kilpatrick, D. Saunders, B. & Smith, W. (2003). Youth Victimization: Prevalence and Implications. *U.S. Department of Justice Office of Justice Programs*. https://www.ncjrs.gov/pdffiles1/nij/194972.pdf

Krüger, C & Fletcher, L. (2017) Predicting a dissociative disorder from type of childhood maltreatment and abuser–abused relational tie, *Journal of Trauma & Dissociation*, 18:3, 356–372, 10.1080/15299732.2017.1295420

Ledesma, J. (2014). *Conceptual frameworks and research models on resilience in leadership. SageOpen, 4*(3), 1–8.

Mambrol, N. (2018, Dec. 19). 'Trauma studies'. Literary theory and criticism. Retrieved from https://literariness.org/2018/12/19/trauma-studies/

Miragoli, S., Camisasca, E., & Di Blasio, P. (2017). Child Sexual Behaviors in School Context: Age and Gender Differences. *Journal of Child Sexual Abuse*, *26*(2), 213–231. https://doi.org/10.1080/10538712.2017.1280866

Solorzano D, Ceja M, & Yosso T. (2000) Critical race theory, racial microaggressions, and campus racial climate: The experiences of African American college students. *Journal of Negro Education*. 69:60–73.

Sotero, M. (2006). A conceptual model of historical trauma: Implications for public health practice and research. *Journal of Health Disparities Research and Practice*, *1*(1), 93–108. https://ssrn.com/abstract=1350062

Substance Abuse and Mental Health Services Administration (SAMHSA) (2014). *SAMHSA's Concept of Trauma and Guidance for a Trauma-Informed Approach.* HHS Publication No. (SMA) 14-4884. Substance Abuse and Mental Health Services Administration.

United States Department of Health and Human Services (HHS) (2023). Engaging People with Lived Experience to Improve Federal Research, Policy and Practice. Office of the Assistant Secretary for Planning and Evaluation. https://aspe.hhs.gov/lived-experience

Walby, S., Armstrong, J., & Strid, S. (2012). Intersectionality: Multiple Inequalities in Social Theory. *Sociology*, *46*(2), 224–240. https://doi.org/10.1177/0038038511416164

Zgoda K, Shelly P, Hitzel S (2016). Preventing retraumatization: A macro social work approach to trauma-informed practices and policies. The New Social Worker. Available at: https://www.socialworker.com/feature-articles/practice/preventing-retraumatization-a-macro-social-work-approach-to-trauma-informed-practices-policies/ (accessed 18 May 2022).

2 Literature Review and Methodology

Emerging Theories of Sexual Trauma

In conjunction with historical trauma, which focuses on the impact of major historical events on survivors of trauma, there are recent understandings of intergenerational trauma and epigenetics that guide current research on how trauma impacts family patterns and biology. Historical trauma theory (Sotero, 2006) examines histories of cultural groups of people that were enslaved, raped, murdered, and continue to be more likely to experience poverty, infant mortality, and poor health outcomes. This theory states that because of the intensity of the historical events that impacted groups of people, their bodies have long-term effects including poor health outcomes, the "keeping" of trauma within their bodies, and toxic stress for generations. Sotero (2006) states that there are four assumptions that uphold historical trauma theory. First, mass trauma is inflicted upon large populations of historically marginalized people by a socially and economically dominant group of people. Second, trauma is not confined to a single event, but it is a progressive consideration over time. Third, the trauma that a large population experiences becomes a universal experience of the people in the population even generations following the event. Fourth, "the magnitude of the trauma experience derails the population from its natural, projected historical course resulting in a legacy of physical, psychological, social and economic disparities that persists across generations" (p. 95). Generations of women of color who are impacted by historical trauma inform our current understanding of intersectionality. Much can be learned about the phenomenological understanding of supporting sexual trauma in schools from the lens of examining the lived experiences of women of color. Historical trauma theory was merged with the phenomenological approach for this study to create an opportunity for scholarship that continues to amplify the voices and the lived experiences of women from historically marginalized groups who have experienced sexual trauma.

According to Marschall (2022), intergenerational trauma has less to do with the traumatic event itself, but more of a family's inability to break familial patterns and habits that may as a result, re-traumatize the individuals

DOI: 10.4324/9781032648668-3

and family systems. It also encompasses individuals who have not directly experienced the trauma themselves, but experience symptoms and the impact of historical trauma. Biologically speaking, according to Jiang et al. (2019), epigenetics refers to a shift in the sequence of DNA as a result of trauma. "Stressful or traumatic events experienced in childhood or adolescence can be driven by a broad range of life events, including but not limited to physical injury, natural disaster, bullying, and childhood maltreatment" (Horner, 2015).

According to this research, individuals who have experienced an Adverse Childhood Experience (ACE) are more likely to experience mental and/or physical health complications as well as early life mortality. The reason childhood trauma has such a significant impact on adult health outcomes is that childhood trauma induces toxic stress. While stress can be categorized into many different categories, the type of stress that is a result of childhood trauma causes long-term stressors on the body and physiological health of the individual (Joëls & Baram, 2009). It is important to recognize that toxic stress can be passed down generationally, especially when considering intergenerational trauma patterns and epigenetics.

The 19th and 20th centuries are when the concept of post-traumatic stress was not just discussed in literary works but was recognized and validated as a true lived experience (Figley et al., 2017). In the late 17th century, trauma was defined as a condition that was a result of physical injury or shock to the human body (Figley et al., 2017). Beginning around the late 19th century, the term trauma was expanded to also include "a psychological response to a catastrophic event" (p. 2).

Bloom (2019), a scholar of trauma theory, discusses the importance of strengthening organizations and systems to be trauma-informed in an effort to decrease the risk of victimization. Bloom challenges all leaders to shift their thinking about their leadership style recognizing that individual trauma survivors and the systems they navigate are very complex and should be treated as such. According to Bloom, the change in systems thinking should start in the healthcare system. Bloom also discusses the need for patient voice and that at the core of trauma-informed care is the ability to honor the experiences reported by the patient to make a well-informed decision about their health.

Coping theory, established by Folkman and Lazarus (1980), defines coping as the ability to utilize internal and external strategies to decrease the stress response that comes with sexual trauma which may lead to poor health outcomes. Coping theory highlights the cognitive and behavioral coping strategies that an individual experiencing stress possesses to lessen its impact. Stress and coping theory is researched based on two categories. The first category considers the response to systemic stress by physiological and psychological mechanisms in the human mind and body (Selye, 1976). The second category deals with the human response to stress based on cognitive psychology (Lazarus, 1991; Smith, 1993). Currently, coping theory is used to determine the likelihood and prevalence of revictimization to suggest new research on revictimization prevention (Macy, 2007). Revictimization reduction is centered around examining community systems that increase perpetration and women's vulnerability. Pittenger et al. (2016) propose the need to implement ecological systems theory to efforts in minimizing the revictimization of sexual trauma for minors. Child sexual abuse causes prolonged negative life outcomes neurobiologically, mentally, behaviorally, academically, and so on. While most current research shares the connections between individual victimization and overall health disparities, Pittenger et al. (2016) suggest that there are larger more systemic challenges that further perpetuate victimization and as a result contribute to health disparities among youth who have endured sexual trauma. In recent history, sexual abuse has been studied from an adult perspective, but the research is clear that there is now a need to view sexual trauma as a public health issue that must be examined from a developmental lens.

Selye's theory of stress states that prolonged resistance to stress will inevitably produce more stress in the form of inflammatory disease and shorter lifespan (Khiron, 2020). Additionally, nonspecifically induced changes in biological systems over a prolonged period of time result in stress. These stressors may be produced by multiple stimulus events that cause long-lasting effects on an individual. Prolonged stressors may cause vasodilation and vasoconstriction of the blood vessels, resulting in psychological and physiological imbalances within the individual. A typical response to stress based on Sely's theory is called General Adaptation Syndrome (GAS). The GAS response is one of many physical and physiological stress responses. The alarm reaction consists of an initial shock stage and a countershock phase. The shock phase releases a surge in adrenaline, excitability, and gastro-intestinal ulcerations. The countershock phase begins defensive systems accompanied by adrenocortical actions, which may lead to a system stage of resistance. In this phase, the shock reaction ends and supposes that the system has become accustomed to the stressor. In addition, in this phase, because of the body's seeming adaptation to the specific stressor, there typically exists the body's inability to adjust to additional or other stressors. The persistence of the countershock phase gives way to physical and physiological exhaustion. While Seyle's theory became the leading research in how scholars understood stress, its downfall was its tendency to categorize all types of stressors into the same processes and assumptions of the theory. As a result, using Sely's work and its inability to be applied to more complex types of stress such as anxiety, threat, or emotional arousal, there was a risk for the theory to lose its scientific value. This research, however, can be considered when examining physical manifestations of stress and trauma for survivors of sexual trauma as a data point when considering interventions and preventative care.

The Impacts of Sexual Trauma

Once the foundational work of relationship building among adults is established, the classroom setting becomes a more fluid and natural way for students to feel safe and seen in the classroom setting. This is helpful in building a triangulation of forces that encourages community-building for students and reinforces school success. Sexual trauma primarily impacts the caregiver-child relationship (Foy et al., 2019; Vlachinos et al., 2020). The work of education is relational in nature (Cole et al., 2005). Part of the reason why it is crucial for educators to gain a better understanding of how to support girls who have experienced sexual trauma is because of the strong emphasis on relationships and community building. The issue of sexual assault is addressed in a variety of ways depending on school culture and the needs of the students. Many girls who have experienced sexual trauma are referred out of school and referred to residential treatment settings or juvenile justice system facilities (Blodgett & Dorado, 2016; Chafouleas et al., 2016). Typically, the majority of young women living in alternative juvenile justice system facilities report having a history of experiences with sexual trauma (Skiba et al., 2016). Additionally, much of the existing research on trauma addresses trauma in general, as opposed to sexual trauma by itself (Blodgett & Dorado, 2016).

Chamberlain et al. (2006) proposed that transitional and developmental challenges for middle school girls are more pronounced for middle school girls in foster care. These girls have often already experienced sexual abuse and are at high risk for unhealthy interactions within relationships. "Cascading negative effects" can be initiated by typical middle school experiences. However, at the other extreme, girls in foster care face a number of common challenges, which include delinquency, substance abuse, mental health problems, and health-risking sexual behaviors. Such high-risk behaviors are often a result of isolation and loneliness post-trauma.

In 2001, the National Trauma Stress Initiative and National Child Traumatic Stress Network were established. In 2013, a national conference between 60 trauma experts created trauma competencies for all trauma-based research (Cook et al., 2014). In the last few years, there has been a tremendous increase in scholarship and research on the impacts of childhood trauma. The numbers of sexual violence are even higher according to Townsend and Rheingold (2013).

> "There is not a single definitive study or meta-analysis that practitioners can point to as the basis for a child sexual abuse prevalence statistic. The field of sexual assault is so vast that while having a wealth of information available is helpful, it is also challenging because many practitioners are using outdated and misleading prevalence statistics that are more than a decade old" (p. 6). As a result, Townsend and Rheingold (2013) compiled national data to centralize more recent information on

the prevalence of sexual assault of children, which will be discussed later in this book. Because of the time that has passed since adult participants, Townsend and Rheingold "exclude all adult self-report studies from the final cohort" (p. 13).

According to researchers including Massachusetts Advocates for Children, the collaboration for childhood trauma intervention with Lesley University and Harvard Law School, childhood trauma impacts academic performance in language and communication, social and emotional communication, and problem solving and analysis. Learning new verbal information over-stimulates the traumatized brain, which causes dysregulation, that is, it causes the brain to constantly regulate itself. This can cause teachers to feel stuck on how to support students and foster neurogenesis and interventions to close the gaps in their learning (Aupperle et al., 2012; Cole et al., 2005; Minahan, 2019). The over-stimulated traumatized brain triggers unpredictable behavior as well as challenges in learning that even the student may have difficulty reporting. As a result, teachers can potentially struggle on how to get to the root of a student's challenge in learning. Unfortunately, this can lead to the teacher feeling incompetent and/or the student feeling incapable. Children who have been traumatized also often have no "internal maps" or executive functioning ability to guide them, which causes them to act instead of plan (Cole et al., 2005). As a result, the teacher-student relationship may become strained as teachers attempt to meet the needs of the traumatized student while the student's behavior may become increasingly difficult and unpredictable.

Trauma and Learning Policy Initiative's goal is twofold: (1) to create a safe environment for child survivors and witnesses of violence and (2) to develop effective strategies for educators to have the training and tools they need to ensure the success of their students. When defining trauma, this collaborative article states that: "trauma is not an event itself, but rather a response to a stressful experience in which a person's ability to cope is dramatically undermined" (TLPI, 2013, p. 18). TLPI researchers give suggestions on how to build trust with a trauma survivor in school. Building positive relationships with teachers which function as a daily substitute for caregivers (usually the caregiver is the child's abuser). Educators and caregivers must increase empathy and understanding by connecting with principal, school counselors, and teacher about the child's history

According to Chafouleas et al. (2016), "contemporary school-based efforts have moved away from these reactive approaches towards prevention-oriented models…in which data are routinely used to identify problems early and monitor response to increasingly intensive services to address needs" (p. 5).

There is a growing body of literature on how discipline is handled in schools and in the juvenile justice system among girls who have been sexually traumatized or are at high risk for sexual trauma (Crable et al., 2013; Saar et al., 2016; Williams et al., 2012).

The Center for Substance Abuse and Mental Health Services Administration (SAMHSA, 2014) stated that many institutions are unaware of their systemic practices that may be re-traumatizing to the members of the system. Morris (2018) proposed that the root cause of more harsh discipline practices among Black girls is the adultification of Black girls. The Annie E. Case Foundation and the Georgetown Law Center on Law on Poverty and Inequality (2017) conducted a study entitled "The adultification of black girls." The findings were that Black girls were perceived as more developed and independent than White girls. The perception of black girls is that they are less innocent than their White peers. Young Black girls were seen as less vulnerable. According to the study, black girls have less need for comfort, nurturing, and protection. Additionally, Morris (2018) stated that by not considering how the current system and structure of school itself can be re-traumatizing to girls, educators miss the mark on the work of education as anti-oppression work. Morris expresses the importance of examining how trauma impacts female sexual trauma survivors in school, and recognizing that the issue of sexual trauma, school experience, and intersectionality are all interconnected. The interconnectedness allows for a rich understanding of how the identity of a girl who has endured trauma should help inform educational practice in general.

There continues to be a need for literature that covers the field of sexual trauma separate from the general overarching "trauma" literature. Continuing to include sexual trauma with general "trauma" will cause practitioners to overlook specific needs that the population has that no other population would benefit from. Blodgett and Dorado (2016) reported that "there is no currently established practice integrating the trauma-informed practices in schools and social emotional learning practices" (p. 23). Although programs currently exist to address sexual assault, the responsibility for children's safety is put on students instead of the adults in their lives. Obviously, teachers believe they must create a safe environment for the children they teach. As Scholes, Jones, Steiler-Hunt, Rolfe, and Pozzebon report, teachers must possess a core understanding of the issue and of best practices if they are to create safe environments.

"Trauma-sensitivity" is defined by the Massachusetts Trauma Learning and Policy Initiative as the ability to teach, advocate for, or work with a child with or without prior knowledge and understanding of their trauma background. TLPI defines "a trauma-sensitive approach to schools" as "weaved into the fabric of the school" and that "an integrated and coordinated approach to service delivery is an essential part of a trauma-sensitive school" (TLPI, 2005, p. 8). A trauma-informed education requires strategic planning with stakeholders, assessment of staff needs, confidential interviewing, linking with mental health professionals, policy review, community-liaison teams, and evaluation of program success. Trauma sensitivity is based on the principle of understanding how to support survivors of trauma in a physically and emotionally safe environment.

After the 2020 COVID pandemic, there was a clear need to explore the prevalence of sexual assault and trauma toward children. As the current research states, while studies have shown a need to identify the impact of trauma on adults, it is imperative to examine the impact of trauma as a public health issue and across the developmental stages of children. The approach of developmental impact of trauma on children is necessary to consider educational approaches to trauma-informed care. Between 2019 and 2021, the newest research on the prevalence, impact, and interventions for girls who have endured sexual trauma informs current perspectives on how to address the problem. The Department of Health and Human Services submitted a report on child maltreatment, neglect, and abuse from the year 2020. The following were their findings:

- The national number of children who received child protective services decreased from fiscal year 2019 with 3,476,000 to fiscal year 2020 with 3,145,000.
- In 2020, a total of 9.6 percent of children were sexually abused and sex trafficked.
- In fiscal year 2019, there were approximately 1,830 deaths of children who were victims of neglect or abuse. This was decreased to approximately 1,750 deaths in fiscal year 2020 of children as a result of abuse or neglect.
- Girls between the ages of 2 and 23 years old make up 88.6% of the national average for sex trafficking in the United States.
- In 2020, approximately 1,750 children died as a result of abuse or neglect.

Trauma intervention practices in schools focus mainly on approaches that are cognitive-behavioral and emphasize stress reduction. Research has shown the effectiveness of behavioral therapies for survivors of trauma (Linehan, 1993; Scheeringa, 2011); however, research has not shown whether or not cognitive-behavioral therapies in schools are linked to the academic achievement of girls who have experienced sexual trauma.

According to the Center for Disease Control and Prevention (CDC, 2012), there are recent facts regarding sexual abuse and trauma among children that present a number of gaps and opportunities for current and future research. Currently, 1 in 4 girls in the United States experience child sexual abuse. Consequences of this problem include but are not limited to sexually transmitted infections, chronic illness, post-traumatic stress disorder, suicidal thoughts, ideations and success, depression, mental health illness, substance abuse, and sexually risky behavior.

Unfortunately, many survivors also become perpetrators of abuse as well which speaks to earlier discussion on the concern of the over-referral of child survivors to criminal justice systems. Current evidence on strategies to prevent child abuse has been established but not yet widely shared. Primary prevention strategies are needed to develop and maintain strong nurturing child-caregiver relationships and environments for child survivors of sexual abuse. Opportunities for future research include the improvement of surveillance and monitoring systems in order to prevent incidents of child sexual abuse, understanding risk factors and protective factors for victimization of youth. There is a need to widely distribute current findings and research to prevent and intervene on behalf of child survivors, as well as any newly discovered strategies to build sustainable support systems for them (CDC, 2012).

The methodology sought to approach this qualitative study, which was through the lens of intersectionality. I utilized this approach to gain a deeper understanding of identity and how it informs self-concept and school experience. The following discussion addresses the methodology of the study.

METHODOLOGY

The rationale for conducting a qualitative-phenomenological study is that first, it is exploratory and open-ended, not confirmatory. Second, there is currently not enough research available about the populations of women reflected in this study and how they are impacted by sexual trauma. Additionally, trauma is complex which leads to the necessity of incorporating multiple perspectives of the phenomenon. Next, there is underrepresentation of historically marginalized populations and their experiences in the literature overall. Last, the use of intersectionality as a framework to understand the complexity of experiences is necessary.

I have designed the following study to answer three guiding questions to support school experiences for female survivors of sexual trauma. The guiding research questions for the study were: *What do sexual trauma survivors recall about their academic and social middle and high school experiences? What systems, factors, and conditions, if any, do survivors report as most supportive in middle and high school? What do survivors of sexual trauma want educators to know based on their lived experiences?*

The following discussion details the methodology of the study and the rationale for the study design. The participants and setting are introduced, and then the instruments and tools utilized to conduct the study are detailed. The latter part of the chapter describes the coding procedures of the study, the role of the researcher, and the delimitations of the study.

Study Design

The purpose of this study was to explore and create an in-depth understanding of the shared lived experience of navigating middle and high school among women who have experienced sexual trauma. I used the procedures recommended by (Creswell, 2007) to guide my thinking and designed this qualitative study using the specific methodology of phenomenology. This method was appropriate for this study because it addressed multiple perspectives on the complex issue of navigating school post-sexual trauma.

Phenomenology scholars, Husserl and Heidegger, pioneered the development of the theory of phenomenology in the early 1900s. Husserl also developed Transcendental Idealism as a branch of phenomenology which highlights that the lived experience is distinguished by the perspective of the individual and not as outsiders or the general population receives them (Welton, 2000).

This qualitative research method is defined by Smith (2018) as a theory that is based on the first-person perspective of one who is experiencing an event. Experience can be divided into many forms of consciousness, such as "perception, imagination, thought, emotion, desire, volition, and action." Phenomenology is based on the essence of the individual and what they report about the truth of their identity and how a particular event impacts their experience. It focuses on how an individual contributes to a social space and how they perceive their experience. In addition to how individuals contribute to a social space, it is also important to recognize how their identity can influence the space.

I listened to the voices of female adolescent survivors of sexual trauma to understand their recollections of middle and high school experiences. The following describes the steps I took to gather data, complete the study, and the relevance of choices I made throughout the process. Additionally, I discuss my approach to ensure participant safety and confidentiality.

Participants, Setting, and Outreach

Participants were eligible for this study if they met the four criteria of the study. The criteria for the study are that participants are willing to discuss their school experiences post-trauma. Participants for the study must also identify as female and a member of a protected class. Participants must also possess the ability to discuss their school experiences without being triggered.

For the purposes of the study, participants were excluded if they did not identify as female or member of a protected class, were unable or unwilling to discuss their school experiences post-trauma, or did not meet any of the eligibility criteria.

The research consisted of gathering data on the lived experience of sexual trauma survivors through 14 in-depth individual interviews. All the survivors were women aged 18 years old and older who are survivors of sexual trauma at a young age and who identify as female. They all agreed to participate in the study and were interviewed remotely.

The first step to gathering and selecting participants for the study was to communicate and advertise the opportunity for study participation by way of social media. I informed participants that the purpose and goal of the study was not to discuss the traumatic event but to discuss their lived experience in school given their trauma. I made this distinction to include participants who were able to separate their school experiences from their traumatic event(s). Participants who were not able to share their experiences without being triggered were not included in the study. The intention was to minimize harm to participants. I also understood that I needed to reiterate to potential participants that the goal was not to trigger them, but that it was to provide a safe space to discuss what they needed in school. I also informed potential participants that this was an opportunity to be part of a collection of stories that can contribute to a growing body of knowledge about what students need in school (from the student perspective) when they have endured sexual trauma.

There were two avenues of outreach that were utilized. Private outreach was utilized to contact women's group leaders to request an opportunity to speak with group members and public outreach (via social media and a public invitation) to allow individuals interested in the study to contact the researcher personally if interested in the study.

For private outreach, I initiated contact with various programs such as women's support groups, girls' mentorship groups, detox centers, rape crisis support groups domestic violence programs, and women's shelters. I initiated contact by reaching out to group leaders and asking if their group would allow me to introduce the study and the opportunity to invite their group members to refer participants to the study. One group leader responded but did not follow up. Shortly after the attempts I made with group leaders, I transferred my correspondence to online platforms and utilized social media to inform survivors about the opportunity to participate in the study. I needed to make this change due to the pandemic and a government-mandated stay-at-home order. The social media groups that focus on the empowerment of trauma survivors that I contacted shared the opportunity with about 30,000 virtual group members on Facebook and Instagram. Of those 30,000 members, 20 women reached out to me to follow up on the opportunity. Of the 20 individuals, 16 agreed to be part of the study. Four individuals either did not maintain contact with me or asked to be withdrawn from the study.

During the introduction of the study, I explained that I am doing this research because I am interested in learning about how sexual trauma impacts academic and social access in school. I invited questions or suggestions to guide me on how to make the study relevant to potential participants and to help me think about how to approach potential participants in a sensitive manner. After providing the information, I provided a flier that announced the study that they may have distributed to individuals in their community. I provided the flier for the women who may want to keep it for their consideration or forward it to others whom they feel might be appropriate for it. I assured them that the whole procedure was confidential and that potential participants would not be forced or coerced into participating. I did not begin or continue conversations with potential participants until they read, agreed to, and signed the consent form. When the signed consent form was sent to me, I began the interview process. Participants were reminded that they could withdraw from the study at any time.

I informed them that they may be contacted to elaborate on some of the experiences they have shared. In the initial contacts, I also focused on asking general questions such as "*What are some of your experiences in school?*" I also asked if they were still interested in participating in the study, what the commitment to participate entailed, and what their availability was.

Criteria for Including Participants in the Sample

The four inclusion criteria for participating in the study were as follows: (1) participants identified as female. While the existing literature is rich with research on how sexual trauma impacts boys, for the purposes of narrowing the scope of the study, participants who identify as female were encouraged to participate in the study. (2) Participants must have experienced some form of sexual assault during their childhood, inside or outside of the school setting. (3) Participants must be adults, that is, over 18 years old. (4) Participants must be willing to discuss their post-trauma school experiences.

In these initial contacts, I took special care to be very patient, show sensitivity, and hear what participants had to say so that everyone who shared their story felt appreciated and knew that their story had added value to the study. I approached this work with the mindset that all of the participant contributions are valuable. There were seven participants whom I contacted for additional sessions. I reiterated that I appreciated all they had done to help thus far and will contact people if I have follow-up questions.

Participants in the study ranged from ages 23 to 63. Participants self-identified their race and ethnicity in most cases as Black, Latina, White, Jewish, and Bi-racial. Location of participants are spread throughout various cities in the United States, and occupations were typically in the field of education with a few participants in the health and medical field with two graduate students. One participant's occupation was in banking, and two were private business owners. One participant reported not having completed formal education.

Criteria for Excluding Participants in the Sample

Individuals who were not survivors of sexual trauma as children were excluded from the study. Because the space of trauma is broad and complex, it was important to specify the kind of trauma being examined and that participants had to be adults recalling their childhood sexual trauma experiences.

Individuals who were opting to participate in the study needed to be willing and able to discuss their school experiences – not discuss or disclose the traumatic event itself. Currently, existing research literature that examines trauma leans toward the field of clinical and psychological counseling. It was important to make clear the purpose of the study and to set the parameters of the study and what was to be discussed.

Last, participants who did not identify as female were excluded from the study based on the complexities of gender as it relates to childhood sexual trauma.

Table 2.1 includes demographic and educational information of each survivor who opted into the research study. While it is not necessary to be specific about names and identifying information of each survivor, it is useful to see trends, connections, and themes having to do with participant demographics, educational backgrounds, and what they reported about their school experiences. I strove to have about 20% of my participants identify as a member of a protected class/underserved population. As seen in the demographic information, 50% of the survivors identify with marginalized populations. Additionally, later in the study, I referred to "(identity)" when asking participants to discuss how their identity intersects with their trauma and their school experiences. I left the term "identity" open to the discretion of the participants.

Table 2.1 Survivor Demographic Information.

Assigned participant pseudonym	*Age*	*Occupation*	*Race; ethnicity; nationality; religion*	*Location*
Daisy	31	Early childhood educator	Black	MA
Rosemary	31	Banking	White	ME
Amaryllis	26	Student/server	White/Hispanic	MA
Azalea	33		White/Christian	MA
Anise	34	Business owner	African American/Christian	NJ
Lilly	63	Disabled	White/Italian	PA
Primrose	29	Teacher	Black	IL, CA
Cora	45	Doctoral student	Black/Pentecostal	AZ
Iris	48	Teacher	White/American/ Christian	NC
Forsythia	23	Front office in internal medicine	American/Jewish	AL
Lavender	61	Occupational therapist	German and Danish ancestry White/Christian	
Lilac	34	Teacher	American/Christian	
Magnolia	56	Teacher	White/English-Scott/Atheist	
Marigold	33	School social worker	White American/Agnostic	
Nerine	30	Teacher (7th grade ELA)	Biracial/Christian	MA

Development of Instruments

This section describes the data collection process for this study. The instruments including interview protocols were designed to capture the complexity of trauma in ways that became essential while analyzing the data. The following data collection approaches were utilized:

- Interviews
- Follow-up interviews
- Analytical notes/memos in field journal

Interviews were opportunities for participants to share their personal stories about how they have experienced school. The selections I made for follow-up interviews were based on themes in participant responses in interview one. Survivors who answered questions in similar ways were likely to be asked for follow-up interviews. This was especially true if their background and personal experiences suggest that their responses should differ from each other. The purpose of the initial interview is to understand the participant's perspective of being a survivor of sexual trauma as it relates to their experience in school. The initial interview will allow me to understand how the expectations that the participants had of their educational experiences may or may not have been met. The focus of the interviews will highlight the lived experience of the participant post-sexual trauma. I utilized this method because of the volume of spoken and written words that I examined and for the purpose of creating new meanings based on the experiences reported by the participants. I wanted to be authentic to what the data showed as a whole while being true to what participants reported as their individually unique experiences.

Follow-up interviews asked probing questions and were used to conduct wellness checks and member checks. These interviews were aided by Creswell's (2014) theory of qualitative research design.

A field journal documented my thoughts, insights, and observations throughout the data collection and analysis process. During interviews, for example, I captured language, tone, body language, emotion, and gestures. I reflected on the complexity of trauma and the experiences that were reported.

The interview protocol (found in Appendix D) was utilized as a product of a protocol creation process proposed by Castillo-Montoya (2016). Castillo-Montoya (2016) developed the Four-Phase Process to Interview Protocol Refinement (IPR). Phase 1 ensures that interview questions are aligned with the research questions. Phase 2 involved constructing an inquiry-based conversation. In phase 3, I consulted with others about the interview protocol. Phase 4 was the piloting and refinement of the interview protocol with a small sample (p. 4). Table 2.2 discusses the purpose of each phase of the protocol creation as indicated by the Castillo-Montoya process.

Table 2.2 Interview Protocol Refinement.

Phase	*Purpose of phase*
Phase 1: Ensuring interview questions align with research questions.	To create an interview protocol matrix to map the interview questions against the research questions.
Phase 2: Constructing an inquiry-based conversation	To construct an interview protocol that balances inquiry with conversation
Phase 3: Receiving feedback on interview protocol by requesting the advice of colleagues and doctoral committee	To obtain feedback on interview protocol
Phase 4: Piloting the interview protocol	To pilot the interview protocol with a small sample to inform final revisions for protocol wording, organization, and procedures.

Note. Adapted from: "Preparing for Interview Research: The Interview Protocol Refinement Framework," by M. Castillo-Montoya (2016), *The Qualitative Report, 21,* p. 811–831. Copyright 2016 by The Qualitative Report.

Interview questions for the study pertained to academic and social engagement during middle and high school years after the experience of sexual trauma, the systems or other conditions that were in place at school that allowed for sexual trauma response to be lessened while at school, and the systems, programs, or other supports that are needed for girls who have experienced sexual trauma. The purpose of the questions was to understand what trauma survivors reported they needed from school in order to thrive academically and socially. Questions were open-ended and focused on keeping the participant feeling safe and secure in sharing their lived experience.

Data Collection Procedures

All participants/survivors who shared their stories informed the study and were useful in helping people gain more understanding of the problem. I ensured that their perspectives were captured in aggregate data that I would report in the data analysis of the study. Participants were chosen from the pool of individuals who had reached out to me individually. Initial phone conversations were conducted with potential participants. Because of the sensitivity of the topic, I reiterated to the participants that the purpose of the study was not to discuss the traumatic event but to understand the experiences and needs of the participants during their middle and high school years in their school setting. Participants were informed about the procedures of the study and that it would entail one or more interviews. Because of the sensitivity of the subject matter and how vulnerable survivors are during discussions, I was careful so that those who participated in the study but were not chosen for second or follow-up interviews did not feel dismissed or rejected.

The data consisted of interview responses from participants in order to gain an understanding of their lived experiences as childhood sexual trauma survivors in their school settings. I initiated contact with potential participants by posting the opportunity to participate on social media (see Appendix B).

1. After the initial contact (potential participant contacts me), I sent them the consent form and requested a time to set up a call to review it together.
2. I then conducted an informal screening to determine their eligibility to participate in the study.
3. Because of the sensitivity of the topic, I reiterated to participants that the purpose of the study is not to discuss the traumatic event but to understand the lived experience and needs of the participants during their school years in their school setting.
4. Participants were informed about the procedures of the study and that it would entail one or more interviews.
5. They were informed that they may be invited for a second interview based on their first interview responses.

Interview settings depended on how the participants reported they would feel most comfortable. Interviews were either over the phone or via video chat or participants wrote down their responses to questions and sent them back to me. Follow-up interviews were conducted if participants had questions and if I recognized that participants could elaborate more on one or more responses to the initial interview. Follow-up interviews were conducted with participants who answered questions similarly. A few participants were asked personalized follow-up interview questions based on the statements they made in their initial interview. Personalized follow-up questions are written directly beneath the participant's response to the initial interview question in my field journal.

Interview Questions

In Table 2.3, I demonstrate how each interview question aligns with the study's guided research questions.

- What is your: Age, Race, Occupation, Nationality, and/or Religion?
- Tell me about your middle and high school.
- How would you classify the type of school(s) you attended?
- As you recall your time in school. What are some experiences that come to mind that can help me understand what school was like for you as a student?
- As you recall your time in school, name a significant interaction(s) or memory(s) that you recall after your traumatic experience
- Were there differences in your school experiences before and after the trauma?

- How did your (identifier) intersect and impact your experience as a sexual trauma survivor in school?
- How did your identity as a woman intersect and impact your social/racial experience as a sexual trauma survivor in school?
- As you recall your school experiences after the traumatic experience, what are some things that were said or done by people at your school that you found helpful?
- As you recall that time in your life after your traumatic experience, what are some things you wish people at school had said or had done that you now think would have helped?
- As you recall your school experience, what are some ways that people at school attempted to be helpful but you wished they did not try?
- Please describe your Academic and Social Experiences
- Do you have any advice about how schools can be helpful to girls who have experienced trauma?

These questions were aligned with the guiding questions because they position participants as the authority on the lived experience in schools as survivors of sexual trauma. Participant responses to questions were meant to highlight their lived experiences in school and allow the researcher to learn how the lived experiences helped to shape identity. Participant recollection serves as the initial source of data for this research. Participant reports of their

Table 2.3 Alignment of Research Questions and Interview Questions.

	Guiding research questions:		*Interview questions:*
1	RQ1:	What do sexual trauma survivors recall about their academic and social middle and high school experiences?	• As you recall your time in school, name a significant interaction(s) or memory(s) that you recall after your traumatic experience • Were there differences in your school experiences before and after the trauma?
	RQ2:	What systems, factors, and conditions, if any, do survivors report as most supportive in middle and high school?	• As you recall your school experiences after the traumatic experience, what are some things that were said or done by people at your school that you found helpful? • As you recall that time in your life after your traumatic experience, what are some things you wish people at school had said or had done that you now think would have helped? • As you recall your school experience, what are some ways that people at school attempted to be helpful but you wished they did not try?
	RQ3:	What do survivors of sexual trauma want educators to know based on their lived experiences?	• Do you have any advice about how schools can be helpful to girls who have experienced trauma?

experiences enhanced current understandings of phenomenology and intersectionality. Because each individual story is different, the questions allow for open-ended honesty about the lived experience. Multiple responses to the questions create a small collection of stories that are likely reflective of lived experience of women outside of the immediate locations of the participants in this study. All participant responses were blinded through a numeric code. All participant responses were electronically password-protected.

Follow-up Interviews, Wellness Checks, and Member Checks

Throughout the study, the member checks and wellness checks allowed me to ensure that you have offered to participate in the study and have not been triggered, felt uncomfortable, or uneasy at any point in the process. I conducted the wellness checks by emailing, calling, and/or checking frequently during the interview(s).

As part of the process for inviting participants to a follow-up interview, I conducted a wellness check to ensure that a follow-up interview would not cause undue harm to the participant. I also repeated two of their specific responses and noted what participants named as personal or challenging to put into words. The purpose for repeating those personal responses back to participants was to acknowledge and thank them for their ability to be vulnerable with me, as well as to gauge the participant's ability to have a follow-up conversation about their experience.

I also followed up with member checks. The purpose of the member checks was to ensure that findings were consistent with participants' lived experiences. Typically, during initial interviews, I frequently conducted member checks with participants for approximately every other question. Before the interview began, I conducted an initial check as well as previewed with participants that I would conduct checks throughout the interview. I also incorporated a final interview question that was geared toward giving participants an opportunity to express their thoughts, feelings, and emotions as a final member check. I made amendments to the interview protocol based on the data and to ensure that I clarified participant statements and perspectives. I also checked in about commonalities in responses and confirmed that I was interpreting their responses correctly. I did this by repeating back to participants what I heard them say and providing space to be corrected by participants if I misinterpreted their responses. I reminded participants during each interview, wellness, and member check that they were able to withdraw from the study at any point.

Memo Reflections

In this work, I reduced bias by examining the data in participant responses and separating their responses from my own lived experiences. I created a written narrative profile of each participant and wrote themes that emerged from all participant responses regarding lived experiences. I created a space for myself to examine the individual and collective experiences of participants to provide more distance between them and my own personal biases and experiences. Having collected data about the overall lived experiences of participants as well as individual experiences enhanced my ability to be unbiased in conducting the research.

Memo reflections were used to write additional analysis of participant responses to interview questions. Reflections included additional thoughts on participant responses as well as similarities in participant responses. For example, all participants although their responses differed were similar enough to be separated into five main categories. These categories were discussed to create themes. The categories were as follows: isolation; race and gender; power and control; identity; and intersectionality. Later in this section, I will discuss how the categories inform the themes in the study.

Data Analysis

The process of understanding and analyzing the data was done systematically and manually. I first developed a personal organization system to maintain a record of memos that were developed from analyzing transcripts. The second stage of analysis was a portion that involved working with words. Third, I identified codes in participant responses and noted them in memos. Next, codes were reduced to literature-based categories or themes. Last, I utilize participant reports on their experiences to create four conglomerate characters and survivor stories representing diversity and point of view of participants in the study. The following describes each step of this data analysis process.

Field-based Memos

First, I developed a personal organization system to maintain a record of memos detailing individual lived experiences of participants to reduce bias. Analytic notes to myself about interview responses created a space to build a new narrative that was driven by participant responses and what was echoed throughout multiple participant responses. This strategy allowed me to further reduce bias while analyzing the data.

The main unit of data analysis was the participants' experiences in school post-trauma. I implemented five of Creswell's (2007) analytic strategies for data analysis. Because this study was established based on the phenomenon of participant experiences, it was most important for me to accurately represent the voices and experiences of participants as much as possible. The memos capture what Minnich (2005) discusses as the importance of how words build common knowledge. The transcripts captured in field notes come directly from the voices and lived experiences of the participants to create a new body of knowledge to begin the conversation of what it is like to be a female sexual trauma survivor in school.

Working with Words

Participants' stories were told using particular words to highlight or color their experiences. Based on Creswell's (2007) recommendations for data analysis, I discuss five ways in which participants used their words to verbally respond to the questions in the interview protocol. The importance of participant use of words is based on the value of each participant's lived experience and what they report about what it was like to be a sexual trauma survivor in school. The goal of learning and preserving participants' lived experiences for the purposes of this study is to be added to the existing body of knowledge that informs how educators and school leaders can be intentional about supporting sexual trauma survivors in school (Blodgett & Dorado, 2016).

After each interview, I examined participant responses to all questions. I observed how participants used words and their language in their responses. Although there were different participants answering the same questions, many of them used words in similar ways depending on the question they were asked. In this first step of the data analysis, I observed the language used and noted patterns and similar language in different participant responses.

The field notes that I took in my memos consisted of analysis of survivor responses to interview questions. I generated categories based on the responses captured from transcriptions in the analytic memos. Responses were grouped into categories that coincided with patterns in their narratives about their school experiences. The patterns that emerged from participant responses included isolation, race and gender, power and control, identity and responses that were consistent with intersectionality theory and how it relates to survivors of sexual trauma. Participant responses about power and control were shared when asked about how identity impacted their school experiences. These responses eventually informed participant reflections about their identity and how their experiences with trauma impacted their identity. These reflections informed my approach in utilizing intersectionality theory to inform how experiences of racism and sexism exacerbate the experience of sexual trauma.

Identifying Codes

I used participant words noted above to create codes to structure their position in their lived experiences and what they reported they needed from their schools while attending. The codes that emerged from the participant responses were extracted from their choices of words and how they managed their language to recreate their lived experiences for each of the questions. Some of the most common codes included participants reporting feelings of loneliness and isolation. These feelings reported by participants align with what is stated in the current literature about the nature of trauma. Additionally, participant responses of feeling invisible, or unseen in school as a result of their trauma also are consistent with existing literature and what participants report as the most prominent feelings post-trauma. Participants also reported being unable to recall academic experiences and/or engage in academic programs in school post-trauma. Much like the similarities I observed in their choices of words in the responses, there were also similarities in patterns in the way they answered. The codes that emerged from the participant responses were pulled from their choices of words and how they managed their language to recreate their lived experiences for each of the questions. Much like the similarities I observed in their choices of words in the responses, there were also similarities in patterns in the way they answered.

After I utilized words and generated codes with attributed structural and descriptive methods. I executed the cycle of coding methods as recommended by Saldaña (2016). First, I developed organizing analytic memos and then attributed structural and descriptive coding methods based on patterns in participant responses. For example, when survivors discussed their individual responses to conflict in school post-trauma, it became clear that there was a psychological impact of trauma that existed for each of them despite the differences in their experiences. Based on this, I developed "a Psychological impact of trauma" as a theme.

Reducing Codes to Themes

From the many codes generated, I carefully reduced them to three themes that became my organization for reporting findings. For relating categories to analytic framework in the literature – the framework that I have used to shape the study – is the study of phenomenology and the value of qualitative research study in the lived experience. I utilized the literature and existing knowledge from Massachusetts Advocates for Children (Blodgett & Dorado, 2016; Cole et al., 2019; Toomey et al., 2008) which served as foundational in understanding how survivors might achieve resilience in their academics and social interactions in school. I utilized this and similar research to inform my research on what we know and what we need to know about supporting sexually traumatized girls in school. For example, when survivors described challenges with identity, despite variations in their reports, it was clear that there was a theme around how trauma impacts identity.

With challenges that come with identity, survivors reported either struggling with fitting into a friend group at school or feeling so insecure about who they were they withdrew and became socially isolated. This necessitated an additional theme not found previously in the literature that there was a "social impact as a result of sexual trauma."

When survivors responded to the interview questions about who they were as students, most of them described feelings of isolation throughout their middle and high school experiences. When asked about the most supportive systems in schools by participants, about 50% of participants tied their feelings of safety and connectedness (in contrast to *survivors often feeling lonely in school*) to an individual teacher or guidance counselor who paid attention to details such as body language, tone, energy, attitude, and behavior. The remaining 50% of participants responded with "nothing," "none," or "N/A," indicating that they did not experience people, systems, or conditions in school that they felt were helpful or made them feel safe in school.

Throughout the interviews, survivors discussed what actions, words, or circumstances they felt would have remedied or lessened the social impact of sexual trauma in school. *Remedy for Social impact* became included as a subcategory after they reflected and shared how their social interactions and relationships could have been fostered in a more intentional and healthy way.

Survivors also discussed what actions, words, or circumstances they felt would have remedied or lessened the psychological impact of sexual trauma in school. *Remedy for Psychological impact* became included as a subcategory that spoke to what survivors felt they needed from the educators and school leaders while managing their trauma in school.

Creating a Point of View

To further understand the data, I utilized participant reports on their experiences to create a point-of-view vignette (Creswell, 2007). I developed four conglomerate characters that represent the diversity of participants in the study. I developed four points of view in an effort to be representative of the various cultural groups by which participants identified. The goal was to capture the intersections of race, gender, and socioeconomic status as reported by participants. Each character was created based on how participants directly addressed how sexual trauma impacts identity and how self-perception impacts the school experience. The four characters I created are introduced in Chapter 4.

The following are the questions that are addressed with each of the four character reflections in creating a point of view:

- *As you recall your time in school. What are some experiences that come to mind that can help me understand what school was like for you as a student?*
- *Describe your academic and social school experiences.*
- *As you recall your time in school, name a significant interaction(s) or memory(s) that you recall after your traumatic experience*
- *How did your (identity) intersect and impact your social/racial experience as a sexual trauma survivor in school?*

It was important to me to ensure that while I extracted an overall point of view from the data, I maintained the integrity of the lived experience of each of the participants individually. I achieved this by reviewing survivor responses and recognizing patterns and similarities within their lived experiences. The patterns and similarities were used as representative of the overall survivor point of view.

Limitations

The limitations of this study are first that as a phenomenological study, it focuses primarily on highlighting the voices and first-hand account experiences of the participants. It does not provide definite causal relationships between sexual trauma survivors in school and academic achievement. Additionally, there were only 15 participants in the study which serves to give insight into some patterns that may exist for sexual trauma survivors psychologically, socially, and academically. It does not serve as a representative for all sexual trauma survivors and their school experiences. Participants are from various parts of the United States but still present a limited perspective in that the study captures survivors from 14 US cities.

The limitations of the study included participant self-identification and acknowledgment of a specific lived experience. Because of the sensitivity of the topic, the study was delimited to adult women who were comfortable sharing their lived experiences as survivors of sexual trauma. Participants in this study were chosen based on requesting the desire to be considered for participation in the study. Participants were asked to recall their school experiences and their needs as student survivors of sexual trauma. Because of the accessibility of myself and participants with social media and telecommunications, the geographical location of where potential participants were located was flexible. Because I have limited the study, I may not have gotten the perspectives of teachers, school personnel, and families of participants. While the lived experiences belong to participants, the perspectives of all caregivers of the survivor may have enhanced understanding an additional perspective to the narrative of participant experiences.

The limitations of the study include the context of each participant, the number of stories gathered within the study, how participants identified, and the level of willingness that they had to share their experience. Each participant came from a different context than the rest of the sample. Additionally, demographic information such as age or race could not serve as representative context for participants who shared similar demographic information. Because context is so specific to each person, there were limitations to how each participant perceived their own context, specifically the context of their school.

While I was intentional in ensuring that the sample size in the study was representative of underserved populations, still the sample size is too small to capture the worldwide dilemma of sexually traumatized girls navigating school post-trauma. The study was also limited because the majority of participants were North American and reported on their experiences in North American school systems.

Another limitation in the study was that participants had to identify as female and had to be willing to discuss and share their school experiences given their sexual trauma. During data collection, interviews were held remotely which allowed for the study to be open to more participants from a broader scope of locations. The limits of the study disallow from one of many potential male perspectives as sexual trauma survivors in school. While I could potentially infer findings based on participant responses, I could not capture the experience of all survivors. The analysis is not meant to make generalizations about the school experience of a sexual trauma survivor. It is meant to provide insight into what survivors in this study reported about their school experiences. It is also meant to provide recommendations to educators and school leaders on how to work together to create a safe and supportive learning environment for survivors of sexual trauma.

Validity

Based on the scholarship on qualitative research, validity is defined as the accuracy of a study as a result of learning the intended concept based on the framework of the research study (Golafshani, 2003). Wainer and Braun (1998) build on this concept by discussing the importance of gathering the intended data set that should confirm the intended hypothesis. The level of validity in this study is based on the level of transparency of the participants when providing their responses to the questions asked of them. While participants reported their level of comfortability in the form of consent and verbal confirmation, there are limits to the level of honesty in participant responses. Additionally, while there are multiple themes, similarities, and connections to participant responses (who are not aware of each other's identity), there may be a discrepancy between participants in this study have chosen to answer questions and how survivors of sexual trauma may have answered questions in general if they were not participating in a research study.

The phenomenological research design was selected to better understand the complexity of trauma by incorporating multiple perspectives and participant memories of the phenomenon. Phenomenology was integrated with intersectionality in this study by creating a space to broaden the meaning of what it means to be a survivor of sexual trauma and how identity is impacted by that experience. Participants of the study utilized their lived experiences to create meaning about how trauma impacts the various aspects of identity. As the researcher, I took great care to respect the participants and the participant narratives. I carefully developed open-ended and focused questions in the interview to keep the participant feeling safe and secure in sharing their lived experiences. The comprehensive design was influenced by Creswell (2007, 2014), Husserl (1931), Smith (2018), and Tufford and Newman (2010). A thorough look at my role as a researcher touches on my own intentions, biases, limitations, and ethical considerations. Chapter 4 will present four composite cases and new learnings that result from the analysis.

References

Aupperle, R., Melrose, A., Stein, M., Paulus, M., (2012). Executive function and PTSD: Disengaging from Trauma. *National Library of Medicine*, 62(2). https://pubmed.ncbi.nlm.nih.gov/21349277/

Blodgett, C., & Dorado, J. (2016). A Selected Review of Trauma-Informed School Practice and Alignment with Educational Practice. http://ext100.wsu.edu/cafru/wpcontent/uploads/sites/65/2015/02/CLEAR-Trauma-Informed-Schools-White-Paper.pdf

Bloom, S. L., & Farragher, B. (2013). *Restoring sanctuary: A new operating system for trauma-informed organizations*. Oxford University Press.

Bloom, S. L. (2019). Trauma theory. In R. Benjamin, J. Haliburn, & S. King (Eds.), *Humanising mental health care in Australia: A guide to trauma-informed approaches* (pp. 3–30). Routledge/Taylor & Francis Group. https://doi.org/10.4324/9780429021923-1

Centers for Disease Control (CDC). (2012). Adverse Childhood Experiences (ACE) Study: Major Findings. http://www.cdc.gov/ace/findings.htm

Center for Substance Abuse Treatment (US). (2014). Trauma-Informed Care in Behavioral Health Services. Rockville (MD): Substance Abuse and Mental Health Services Administration (US). (Treatment Improvement Protocol (TIP) Series, No. 57.) Chapter 1, Trauma-Informed Care: A Sociocultural Perspective. https://www.ncbi.nlm.nih.gov/books/NBK207195/

Chafouleas, S. M., Johnson, J. H., Overstreet, S., & Santos, N. M. (2016). Toward a blueprint for trauma-informed service delivery in schools. *School Mental Health*, *8*, 144–162. https://doi.org/10.1007/s12310-015-9166-8

Chamberlain, P., Leve, L. D., & Smith, D. K. (2006). Preventing behavior problems and health risking behaviors in. *International Journal of Behavioral Consultation and Therapy*, *2*(4). http://files.eric.ed.gov/fulltext/EJ804058.pdf

Cole, S.F., O'Brien, J. G., Gadd, M. G., Ristuccia, J., Wallace, D.L., Gregory, M. (2005) *Helping traumatized children learn: Supportive school environments for children traumatized by family violence*. Massachusetts Advocates for Children.

Cook, A., Blaustein, M., Spinazzola, J., & van der Kolk, B. (Eds.). (2003). *Complex trauma in children and adolescents*. National Child Traumatic Stress Network. http://www.NCTSNet.org

Cook, J. M., Newman, E., & the New Haven Trauma Competency Group. (2014). A consensus statement on trauma mental health: The new haven trauma competency conference process and major findings. *Psychological Trauma: Theory, Research, Practice, and Policy*, *6*, 300–307. http://dx.doi.org/10.1037/a0036747

Coster, W., & Cicchetti, D. (1993). Research on the Communicative Development of Maltreated.

Crable, A. R., Underwood, L. A., Parks-Savage, A., & Maclin, V. (2013). An examination of a gender-specific and trauma-informed training curriculum: Implications for providers. *International Journal of Behavioral Consultation and Therapy*, *7*(4), 30–37.

Creswell, J. W. (2007). *Qualitative Inquiry and Research Design: Choosing among Five Approaches* (2nd ed.). Thousand Oaks, CA: Sage Publications.

Creswell, J. W. (2013). *Qualitative inquiry & research design: Choosing among five approaches* (3rd ed.). SAGE.

Creswell, J. W. (2014). *Research Design: Qualitative, Quantitative and Mixed Methods Approaches* (4th ed.). Thousand Oaks, CA: Sage.

Figley, C. R., Ellis, A. E., Reuther, B. T., & Gold, S. N. (2017). The study of trauma: A historical overview. In S. N. Gold (Ed.), *APA handbook of trauma psychology:*

Foundations in knowledge (pp. 1–11). American Psychological Association. https://doi.org/10.1037/0000019-001

Folkman, S., & Lazarus, R. S. (1980). An analysis of coping in a middle-aged community sample. *Journal of Health and Social Behavior, 21*, 219–239. https://doi.org/10.2307/2136617

Foy, J., Green, C., & Earls, M. (2019). Psychological aspects of child and family health. *Mental Health Competencies for Pediatric Practice. Pediatrics, 144*(5), e20192757.

Herman, J. (1992). Complex PTSD: A syndrome in survivors of prolonged and repeated trauma. *Journal of Traumatic Stress. 5*(3), 377–391. https://doi.org/10.1002/jts.2490050305

Hill Collins, P. (2000). *Black feminist thought: Knowledge, consciousness, and the politics of empowerment* (2nd ed.). Routledge Press.

Horner G. (2015). Childhood trauma exposure and toxic stress: what the pnp needs to know. *J Pediatr Health Car* 29(2):191–8. doi: 10.1016/j.pedhc.2014.09.006

James, B. (1994). *Handbook for treatment of attachment-trauma problems in children.* Simon and Schuster.

Jiang, S., Postovit, L., Cattaneo, A., Binder, E. B., & Aitchison, K. J. (2019). Epigenetic modifications in stress response genes associated with childhood trauma. *Front. Psychiatry, 10*, 808. https://doi.org/10.3389/fpsyt.2019.00808

Joëls, M., & Baram, T. Z. (2009). The neuro-symphony of stress. *Nature reviews. Neuroscience, 10*(6), 459–466. https://doi.org/10.1038/nrn2632

Macy, R. J. (2007). Sexual Revictimization: Implications for Social Work Practice. *Families in Society, 88*(4), 627–636. https://doi.org/10.1606/1044-3894.3685

Minahan, J. (2019). Trauma-Informed Teaching Strategies. *Educational Leadership. 77*(2). http://www.ascd.org/publications/educational_leadership/oct19/vol77/num02/Trauma-Informed_Teaching_Strategies.aspx

Morris, M. W. (2018). *Pushout: the criminalization of Black girls in schools.* New York, The New Press.

Ngo, V., Langley, A., Kataoka, S. H., Nadeem, E., Escudero, P., & Stein, B. D. (2008). Providing evidence-based practice to ethnically diverse youths: Examples from the cognitive behavioral intervention for trauma in schools (CBITS) program. *Journal of the American Academy of Child and Adolescent Psychiatry, 47*(8), 858–862. https://doi.org/10.1097/CHI.0b013e3181799f19

Saar, M. S., Epstein, R., Rosenthal, L., & Vafa, Y. (2016). The sexual abuse to prison pipeline: The Girls' story. *Georgetown Law: Center on Poverty and Inequality.* https://nowpbc.files.wordpress.com/2013/04/2015_cop_sexual-abuse_layout_web-1.pdf

Saldaña, J. (2016). *The coding manual for qualitative researchers* (3rd ed.). SAGE.

Scheeringa, M. S., Weems, C. F., Cohen, J. A., Amaya-Jackson, L., & Guthrie, D. (2011). Trauma-focused cognitive-behavioral therapy for posttraumatic stress disorder in three-through six year-old children: a randomized clinical trial. *Journal of Child Psychology and Psychiatry, and Allied Disciplines, 52*(8), 853–860. https://doi.org/10.1111/j.1469-7610.2010.02354.x

Selye, H. (1976). Stress without Distress. In: Serban, G. (eds) Psychopathology of Human Adaptation. Springer, Boston, MA. https://doi.org/10.1007/978-1-4684-2238-2_9

Substance Abuse and Mental Health Services Administration (SAMHSA) (2014). *SAMHSA's Concept of Trauma and Guidance for a Trauma-Informed Approach.* HHS Publication No. (SMA)14-4884. Substance Abuse and Mental Health Services Administration.

Shonkoff, J. P., Garner, A. S., & Committee on Psychosocial Aspects of Child and Family Health, Committee on Early Childhood, Adoption, and Dependent Care, & Section on Developmental and Behavioral Pediatrics. (2012). *The lifelong effects of early childhood adversity and toxic stress. Pediatrics*, *129*(1), e232–e246. https://doi.org/10.1542/peds.2011-2663

Skiba, R. J., Artiles, A. J., Kozleski, E. B., Losen, D. J., & Harry, E. G. (2016). Risks and consequences of oversimplifying educational inequities: A response to Morgan et al. (2015). *Educational Researcher*, *45*(3), 221–225. https://10.3102/0013189X16644606

Smith, D. W. (2018). Phenomenology. *The Stanford Encyclopedia of philosophy* https://plato.stanford.edu/archives/sum2018/entries/phenomenology.

Sotero, M. (2006). A conceptual model of historical trauma: Implications for public health practice and research. *Journal of Health Disparities Research and Practice*, *1*(1), 93–108. https://ssrn.com/abstract=1350062

Toomey, A., Brennan, E. M., & Friesen, B. (2008). Resilience Theory as a Framework for Teaching Human Development within HBSE. http://www.rtc.pdx.edu/PDF/pbResilienceTheory.pdf

Townsend, C., & Rheingold, A. A. (2013). Estimating a child sexual abuse prevalence rate for practitioners: A review of child sexual abuse prevalence studies. *Darkness to Light*. www.D2L.org/1in10.

Van der Kolk, B. A. (2005). Developmental trauma disorder. *Psychiatric Annals*, *35*(5), 401–408.

Vlachos, I. I., Papageorgiou, C., & Margariti, M. (2020). Neurobiological trajectories involving social isolation in PTSD: A systemic review. *Brain Sci* 10, 173. https://doi.org/10.3390/brainsci10030173

Welton, D. (2000). *The Other Husserl: The Horizons of Transcendental Phenomenology*. Indiana University Press.

Williams, W., Karlin, T., & Wallace, D. (2012). Project SisterCircle: Risk, Intersectionality and Intervening in Urban Schools. *Journal of School Counseling*. http://files.eric.ed.gov/fulltext/EJ981197.pdf

Appendix B

Social Media Outreach (Public Outreach Strategy)

"Examining the Voices of Sexual Trauma Survivors
and their School Experiences"

Are you a survivor of sexual trauma? Would you be interested in sharing your lived experience in school?

I am a doctoral student in Lesley's Educational Leadership program, and I am conducting a research study to learn about the lived experience of women who have experienced sexual trauma. In particular, I would like to know beneficial school practices for childhood sexual trauma survivors.

Below are the eligibility criteria for the study:

- Identify as female
- Are 18 years old and over
- Have experienced some form of sexual assault prior to age 18 inside or outside of the school building.
- Are comfortable discussing lived experience in school post-trauma.

If you are interested, please contact me.
Here is some additional information:

- Participation involves 1-2 audio recorded interviews with me.
- Interviews will be about 45-60 minutes each and will occur via phone/audio, or video call
- Your identity and your responses to my questions will remain confidential.
- There is no compensation for participating in this study.
- There are no direct benefits. However, your participation in this study may provide more information to benefit girls who have experienced childhood sexual trauma and need support in their schools.

If you are interested in being considered for this study, I can be reached by cell at (978) 204-3277, at jetesse@lesley.edu, Jennifer Herring on Facebook or Instagram. If you know someone that fits this description please feel free to forward this announcement

Thanks!

Appendix D

Instrument for Collecting Data- Interview Protocol

"Examining the Voices of Sexual Trauma Survivors
and their School Experiences"

My goal is to hear the school experiences of women who have experienced sexual trauma. Everything we discuss will be confidential. Identifying characteristics will be changed in the reporting of the study findings. My goal as the researcher is to remain neutral toward participant responses at all times during the study. As a participant, you have the right to refrain from answering any questions and withdraw from the study at any time. I will make it clear to potential participants that the study is optional, confidential and that everything will be done to ensure confidentiality and anonymity throughout the whole process.

It will also be reiterated to participants that the purpose of this study is not to discuss their traumatic experience or event, but that the purpose is to gain an understanding of what they report they needed and appreciated about their school experience given their trauma. I would reduce the risk by ensuring that even if participants feel that discussing their school experience would trigger emotions that revive traumatic memories participants would be encouraged to withdraw themselves from participating in the study. Participants will be reassured that they may decline to answer any question, pause or stop an interview session, or withdraw from participation in the study at any time. There is no consequence for withdrawal from the study. Participants who request to pause or discontinue the interview will be provided with resources.

Table 3 Types of Interview Questions for Interview 1

Type of Question	*Main Questions*	*Possible Follow Up Questions*
Demographic Questions	Tell Me About Yourself (Age, Race, Ethnicity, Occupation, Religion, Family Structure).	
Introductory Questions	Tell me about your middle and high school? As you recall your time in school. What are some experiences that come to mind that can help me understand what school was like for you as a student?	How would you classify the type of school(s) you attended? How many years of schooling did you have at each type of school you attended? *(create a time line)* What are some things that come to mind about your academic experiences? What comes to mind about your social experiences?
Transition Questions	As you recall your time in school, name a significant interaction(s) or memory(s) that you recall after your traumatic experience Were there differences in your school experiences before and after the trauma? How did your (identifier) intersect and impact your experience as a sexual trauma survivor in school? How did your identity as a woman intersect and impact your social/racial experience as a sexual trauma survivor in school?	How did the ways that students and teachers interact with each other in school make you feel safe or unsafe during your school experiences? Was your school ever a safe place for disclosing your trauma to a peer or school personnel?
Key Questions	As you recall your school experiences after the traumatic experience, what are some things that were said or done by people at your school that you found helpful? As you recall that time in your life after your traumatic experience, what are some things you wish people at school had said or had done that you now think would have helped? As you recall your school experience, what are some ways that people at school attempted to be helpful but you wished they did not try?	What are some things that come to mind about your academic experiences? What comes to mind about your social experiences? If asked by participant if I mean people who were aware of trauma I would respond with *"yes, people who knew about your trauma, as well as people who did not know."*
Closing Questions	Before we close this interview, is there anything else you'd like me to know about your K-12 school experience? Do you have any advice about how schools can be helpful to girls who have experienced trauma? Any final feedback/suggestions about the experience. Temperature check.	Any final follow up questions that speak to the participant's academic *and* social experiences in school.

(*Note.* Interview protocol created incorporating suggestions from: "Preparing for Interview Research: The Interview Protocol Refinement Framework," by M. Castillo-Montoya, 2016, *The Qualitative Report, 21* p. 811–831. Copyright 2016 by The Qualitative Report)

3 Intersectionality

Introduction

Very few areas in the literature specify the educational needs of sexually traumatized girls. Most of the literature reports best practices in support of students who have experienced general trauma. Trauma intervention practices in schools focus mainly on approaches that are cognitive-behavioral and emphasize stress reduction. These approaches are useful because research has shown the need for behavioral therapies for survivors of trauma (Foa et al., 1991; Scheeringa et al., 2011); however, they may not be useful in helping sexual trauma survivors access academic needs that still exist in school.

Chapter 3 describes how the chapter is organized and how each section discusses data collected to answer the guiding research questions. Next, the chapter discusses the data analyzed for each of the three guiding research questions. Following the discussion of the data analyzed, themes in the guiding research questions are discussed. Last, guiding research question findings are examined.

Relationship between Study Themes and Guiding Research Questions

The themes addressed what survivors reported about the needs of sexual trauma survivors in school. The guiding questions seek to bring understanding about the complexities of intersectionality, sexual trauma, and school experiences. The study seeks to amplify the voices of female survivors of sexual trauma that typically would not otherwise be heard. Much like what is reflected in the academic literature on trauma, survivor reports shared the three findings of the study which are used to bring clarity to additional identity markers for female sexual trauma survivors.

Themes of Impact

The themes are that survivors reported a psychological, social, and academic impact as a result of sexual trauma. The themes that emerged in this study

DOI: 10.4324/9781032648668-4

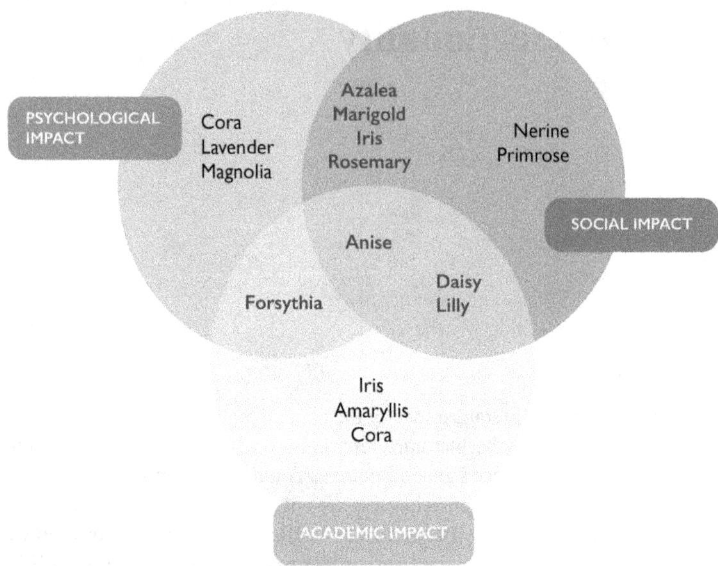

Figure 3.1 The impacts of sexual trauma.

answer the guiding research questions because they are based on psychological, social, and academic challenges of sexual trauma survivors in school. They also are reflective of the clear need for research on the multifaceted impacts of sexual trauma as stated in Chapter 1. Intersectionality theory (Crenshaw, 1994) describes the challenges that women face as they navigate oppressive systems in society while navigating the complexities of their identity. Trauma in its complexity causes each survivor to respond to it differently. Identity is necessary to understanding trauma because it confirms the work of intersectionality theory in that it adds value to the multifaceted identities of survivors as well as how to navigate school given the experience of sexual trauma (Figure 3.1 and Table 3.1).

Intersectionality Theory

Intersectionality theory (Crenshaw, 1989; Walby et al., 2012) is an area of literature that was examined in this study because of the multi-layered experiences and the impacts it has on the individual. It is defined as multiple inequalities manifested in multiple identities in one individual or group of individuals. This theory has historically been focused on the stories of Black women and how the rise of criticism on racial and gender intolerance has grown into the need to examine the multifaceted meaning of being a woman, a

Table 3.1 Themes that Emerged from Interviews.

Theme		*Categories*
Survivors reported on the psychological impact of sexual trauma	a	Survivors report feeling invisible in school.
	b	Survivors reported feeling lost or unable to engage in school
	c	Survivors reported internal struggle
	d	Survivors reported challenges in emerging identities
Survivors reported a social impact of sexual trauma	a	Survivors reported feeling isolated in school
	b	Survivors did not have meaningful connections with family or friends
	c	Survivors reported being labeled as deviant and were misunderstood
	d	Survivors reported feeling silenced in school.
Survivors reported an academic impact of sexual trauma	a	Survivors reported a drastic change in their grades (usually a decrease) after the traumatic event.
	b	Survivors reported an inability to remain engaged academically
	c	some differences before and after trauma, and
	d	Survivors could not recall meaningful academic school experiences.

woman of color, as well as a variety of identifiers that may or may not be tolerated. Crenshaw (1989) and Hill Collins (2000) introduced the term "intersectionality." It is the idea that multiple aspects of oppression (e.g., race, gender and economic status) cannot be seen as separate issues because the oppression itself comes from an intersection of prejudicial ideas that affect multiple aspects of the histories of women of color. Hill Collins stated that "cultural patterns of oppression are not only interrelated, but are bound together and influenced by the intersectional systems of society, such as race, gender, class, and ethnicity…it is interlocking oppression" (Collins, 2000, p. 42).

Crenshaw (1989) and Collins (2000) introduced the term "intersectionality." It is the idea that multiple aspects of oppression (Black, female, etc.) cannot be seen as separate issues because the oppression itself comes from an intersection of prejudiced ideas that affect multiple aspects of the histories of Black women. Hill Collins (2000) stated that "cultural patterns of oppression are not only interrelated, but are bound together and influenced by the intersectional systems of society, such as race, gender, class, and ethnicity…it is interlocking oppression" (p. 42).

Once the foundational work of relationship-building among adults is established the classroom setting becomes a more fluid and natural way for students to feel comfortable and seen in the classroom setting. This is helpful in building a triangulation of forces that encourages community building for students and reinforces academic achievement and school success. Many schools have protocols to address disclosures based on their state laws but often refer sexually assaulted young women to the Department of Children and Families from a fear or hesitation to get involved. Obviously, because sexual assault is ubiquitous, schools must be more intentional about providing safe spaces for disclosures because state laws for sexual assault differ from the laws that protect children from sexual assault.

As a researcher, I recognize that my sociocultural perspective has allowed me to make meaning of the experiences and people that I have encountered. I have also learned to examine social and cultural forces that are at play not just in my perspective but for those who do not share my sociocultural perspective. An effective researcher must understand the various layers that incorporate one person, idea, theory, or problem. While one circumstance can be examined through the lens of my sociocultural perspective, that same circumstance can be examined from a different lens by an individual who does not share my perspective. An approach utilizing the theory of intersectionality would allow me to begin approaching these issues and equip me to be more articulate about the struggle that I experienced as well as how it may be affecting students that I come into contact with within American school systems. All of my personal experiences have been multi-layered and each layer brings a different challenge, question, and opportunity for inquiry. This multi-layered approach to research will allow me to become well-rounded and well-informed as I approach various complex problems as an educator and educational scholar.

Although I remain interested in learning about trauma and its impact on children, I have a particular interest in learning how sexual trauma impacts the school experiences of adolescent girls. I am interested in understanding what sexually traumatized girls need in school to remain engaged academically and socially and how, according to sexually traumatized young women, school conditions and efforts by educators helped them or could have helped them in their academic and social engagement in school.

The framework that I have used to shape the study is the study of phenomenology and the value in qualitative research study in the lived experience. Intersectionality theory (Crenshaw, 1994) describes the challenges that women face as they navigate society with multiple facets of their identity in the midst of oppression. Trauma in its complexity causes each survivor to respond to it differently. Identity is necessary to understanding trauma because it confirms the work of intersectionality theory in that it adds value to the multifaceted identities of survivors as well as how to navigate school given the experience of trauma.

The issue of sexual assault among girls is addressed in a variety of ways in school depending on school culture and the needs of the students. The diverse needs of students are what solidifies the enhancement of the existing intersectionality theory in that it adds an additional layer to what it means to be a sexual trauma survivor. The identity is not just the identification with sexual trauma but also how one learns – internalizes academic information, synthesizes and interprets it. How the student lives out their academic learning is also part of their identity which in essence adds to the concept of intersectionality as a theoretical framework.

Data analysis for this study supported understanding of bridging the gap between survivor-lived experiences and how educators can meet the academic and social needs of their female students who have experienced sexual trauma. Below are the findings of the analysis of the interview data of participants who answered questions about their lived experiences in school after having experienced sexual trauma.

Intersectionality theory framed the analysis of how sexual trauma survivors navigate the school environment. Below are three survivor stories that are based on the stories and experiences of the 14 study participants. The diversity of experiences as well as the similarities of how trauma impacted them are reflective of the complexity of trauma while also showing similarities in survivor stories as well as the various aspects of their identity and how they intersect with the experience of trauma.

When I first heard Rose and other participants share their stories, I was moved by how reflective they were. Participants were able to speak in a very clear and detailed way about their experiences while still maintaining a child-like perspective which added to the authenticity of their reports of their lived experiences. I began to feel sympathetic and empowered at the same time as participants unknowingly walked me through a discreet tale of their traumatic event, how they managed their trauma given all the forces at work in school, and how they overcame the weight of their trauma or worked toward addressing it in their adult life. According to the literature, existing research on supporting sexually traumatized students in school is fragmented (Helge, 1992; King, 1983; Chamberlain et al., 2006). Much like the literature, participants began to share memories and stories that in many cases created a substantial volume of data with what seemed like a lack of cohesion and linear pattern. Initially, it was difficult for me to create cohesion in survivor stories in an effort to undo the fragmentation that exists both in the literature and in their stories. After reflecting on the guiding questions and the purpose of the study, I repeated my review of survivor responses and looked more deeply at the patterns that discussed the impact of trauma and how they managed social and academic experiences in school post-trauma.

The following discussion reveals how survivors lived experiences enhance the discourse on the experiences of sexual trauma survivors at school. First, I discuss the results of the study presented in the form of themes, each with identified categories and illustrative quotes. The themes that emerged in this study answer the guiding research questions because they are based on psychological, academic, and social challenges of sexual trauma survivors in school. They also are reflective of the multifaceted aspects of the existing academic literature on trauma because of the complexity of trauma itself. Survivors also share their insights on remedies that could help mitigate the effects while in school of sexual trauma. According to Chafouleas et al. (2016) and

Blodgett and Dorado (2016), many sexually traumatized girls are referred out of school and to residential treatment settings or juvenile justice system facilities. Typically, a number of young women living in alternative juvenile justice system facilities report having a history of experiences with sexual trauma (Skiba et al., 2016). Additionally, much of the existing research on trauma addresses trauma in general, as opposed to sexual trauma by itself (Blodgett & Dorado, 2016). Based on the literature on how trauma impacts learning (Coster & Cicchetti, 1993), it is likely that girls who have been impacted by sexual trauma will have a unique challenge in their school journey. The current literature on trauma and learning focuses on general trauma as a whole (Cole et al., 2005) rather than how sexual trauma impacts learning. Research that is specifically focused on how sexual trauma impacts learning is generally understood in the context of juvenile justice programs and not K-12 school settings (Blodgett & Dorado, 2016; Skiba et al., 2016).

In the literature about trauma-sensitive practices in schools, it is suggested that educators be trained on how to provide a supportive learning environment for students who have experienced trauma (Blodgett & Dorado, 2016; Cole et al., 2005). Trauma-sensitive practices will inform the study by allowing me to utilize participants' stories to see if their positive school experiences were as a result of their schools adopting the recognized trauma-sensitive approaches or variations of them. I would imagine that participants will also report positive experiences that do not include the recognized trauma-sensitive practices. It will be informative to utilize the stories of positive school experiences that participants share and compare and contrast them with what the literature suggests. Some of the themes that are apparent in the literature include harsh discipline practices typically targeted at girls of color and students who have experienced trauma (Morris et al., 2015; Skiba et al., 2016). Participant reports in the study will be useful in determining whether or not their school experiences align with what the literature describes as a lack of knowledge on how to better address misbehaviors as a result of trauma in the inclusive classroom setting (Blodgett & Dorado, 2016; Chafouleas et al., 2016). Off-task behaviors in school such as inattentiveness, being aloof, withdrawn, and disengaged, even though less obvious, are a result of trauma that may get overlooked. Not all challenging behaviors manifest one way. Resilience Theory, especially its application to educational settings, serves as foundational in understanding how survivors might achieve resilience in their academics and social interactions in school (Toomey et al., 2008). This focus introduces insights into what resilience in an academic setting entails. It is important to hear the perspective of young women to understand what was necessary for them to access the curriculum in school and be able to have healthy social interactions.

Table 3.2 is a recreation of a table that appears in the Townsend and Rheingold (2013) study conducted to present the prevalence of trauma resulting from sexual assault nationwide. This table highlights studies that examine

Table 3.2 Prevalence of Sexual Abuse.

Abuse period studied	*Study known as*	*Prevalence; sample size*
1935–1995	The ACE Study 1995–1997	22%; 13,494
1982–2000	Teen Dating Violence Study 2000–2001	13.2%; 2,101
1917–1995	The National Violence Against Women Study 1995–1996	9.7%; 16,005
1984–2001	School Sports in Adolescents Study 2001	7.3%; 50,168
1988–2005	Adolescent Alcohol-Related Sexual Assault Study 2005	54.1%; 1,017
1978–1995	National Survey of Adolescents 1995	8.2%; 3,614
1986–2003	Developmental Victimization Survey 2003	6.7%; 2,030
1984–2001	Influences of Immigration and Acculturation Study 2001, 2003	14%; 5,919

Adapted from: Townsend and Rheingold (2013).

populations that include adolescent girls and their responses to sexual assault experiences.

In addition to Townsend and Rheingold (2013), various scholars report on the prevalence of sexual assault of women and girls on a national level. Adolescent Alcohol-Related Sexual Assault Study included questions about sexual acts that perpetrators did not considered abusive. Large numbers of abused women likely mean large numbers of abused children. Based on the data compiled, Townsend and Rheingold (2013) concluded the following:

> One in ten children are sexually abused before they turn 18.
>
> As many as 400,000 babies will be sexually abused by their 18th birthday unless we do something to stop it.
>
> (p. 21)

The Rape, Abuse and Incest National Network (RAINN) reports national statistics on sexual abuse in the United States provided by the Bureau of Justice Statistics. Between 2009 and 2013, child protective services agencies reported that 63,000 children a year were victims of sexual abuse. Additionally, one in nine girls experienced sexual assault compared to one in fifty-three boys (Truman & Langton, 2014). The literature establishes that a large portion of incidents of sexual assault take place in a young woman's home (Kilpatrick et al., 2003; Landreth, 2012).

In reviewing the literature, periodically there are instances where rates of sexual assault are severely underreported, as well as periods of time when they are reported at the typical rate. When it comes to criminal victimization, Truman and Langton (2014) reported that there was no significant change in rates of crime from 2013 to 2014. Based on my review of the literature, there continued to be a need for an explanation for years where there is no assault documented as being reported.

Based on the current existing work of the Adverse Childhood Experiences (ACE) studies that have been conducted, it was discovered that the individuals whose experiences were examined were that of White affluent individuals. As a result, the Philadelphia ACE study examined averse experiences of children that reflect the needs and lived experiences of the individuals. Experiences examined in the study include violence, foster care involvement, bullying, safety, and security of the physical environment. Out of the study came numerous studies that examine the impact of trauma and stress on children and adults (ACE Awareness Foundation, 2014; Cronholm et al., 2015). Scholars recognize the need to examine stress and trauma from the perspective of the survivor. They also realize that individuals in historically marginalized groups often are not provided with opportunities to center their voice and lived experiences to bring about systemic change in spaces that should be constructed to consider the relationship between intersectionality and trauma.

Since the COVID-19 pandemic, national responders to child abuse and safety have begun using digital platforms to capture reports of sexual abuse as well as those that typically go unreported otherwise. In 2022, RAINN reported that there were approximately 32 million reports of sexual abuse and sexual exploitation of children. (National Center for Missing & Exploited Children, 2022). There remains to be a need to identify more accurate numbers of how many children are impacted by sexual assault and exploitation, who the children are individually and collectively, as well as what are the educational and political interventions that need to be implemented to educate the larger population on how to prevent and intervene on this issue.

Sexual Exploitation of Children

According to Banks & Kyckkelhahn (2011) at the Department of Justice, 82% of the nation's incidents of human trafficking occurred between 2008–2010. This included over 1,000 reports made by children (Banks & Kyckkelhahn, 2011). Unfortunately, there is a global impact of sex trafficking among underaged girls and a lack of public awareness on the issue. Because of this, girls who are often caught in the midst of a transaction are often legally charged for selling sex and/or additional crimes involved (Coakley & Lloyd, 2008). Because of a lack of awareness and education, many communities charge girls with similar charges as adult women engaging in sex work, and as a result, there was a push toward decriminalizing child sex prostitution (Scheeringa et al., 2011). By 2012, the state of Massachusetts established the Safe Harbor Law, which rather than charging minors with sex crimes referred them to appropriate services necessary for support. The Safe Harbor Law protects

- History of abuse
- Undocumented citizenship status
- Family or personal substance abuse
- Unaccepted/rejected LGBTQ+ youth
- Low self-esteem or self-worth
- Physical or developmental disabilities
- Low socio-economic status
- Unstable/unsafe home environment
- Trauma-related mental health issues
- Lack of support system & basic needs
- Gang association or involvement
- Lack of physical or online supervision
- Using words like "Daddy," "The Life," "Trick/Date", "Track/Blade," "Wifey"
- Involvement with foster care, probation, etc.

Figure 3.2 Risk factors.

children from Commercial Sexual Exploitation and prevents legal action which typically criminalizes the children rather than the adults responsible. According to the United States Office of Juvenile Justice and Delinquency Prevention (2014), commercial sexual exploitation consists of sexual abuse and remuneration in money, goods, or services or the promise of money, goods, or services to the child or a third person or persons (Figure 3.2).

Unfortunately, as Williams et al. (2012) note, Sexual Response to Violence (SRV) has evolved into becoming part of the sexual development of many Blacks and Latinas, and SRV leads to school dropouts, which translates to financial insecurity and a failure to attain educational/career aspirations. If these communities remain under-sourced, they compromise vitality and ability to support optimal development of girls (Lee & Newberg, 2005).

As Skiba et al. (2016) research notes, a growing number of girls enter the juvenile justice system. Many of these girls have experienced sexual/physical abuse, mental health challenges, and neglect. Without trauma-informed and gender-specific interventions in schools, the population will likely experience high rates of criminality, substance abuse, interpersonal violence, and teenage pregnancy.

Of his 48 admitted victims, 27 of them were between the ages of 15 and 18 years old and were practicing sex workers. Figure 3.3 illustrates how the demand for children feeds the supply in the Commercial Sexual Exploitation of Children (CSEC) industry.

The connection between recruiting young women for prostitution and sexual trauma is clear. Young women who have been raised in homes where domestic violence is a norm are conditioned to accept maltreatment and abuse from males in romantic relationships. The role of the pimp or recruiter is to seduce young women who have witnessed sexual violence at home and/or have been sexually assaulted by offering companionship and money. These

THEME	CATEGORIES
SURVIVORS REPORTED on the psychological impact of sexual trauma	a). Survivors report feeling invisible in school. b). Survivors reported feeling lost or unable to engage in school c). Survivors reported internal struggle d). Survivors reported challenges in emerging identities
SURVIVORS REPORTED a social impact of sexual trauma	a). Survivors reported feeling isolated in school b). Survivors did not have meaningful connections with family or friends c). Survivors reported being labeled as deviant and were misunderstood d). Survivors reported feeling silenced in school.
SURVIVORS REPORTED an academic impact of sexual trauma	a). Survivors reported a drastic change in their grades (usually a decrease) after the traumatic event. b). Survivors reported an inability to remain engaged academically c). some differences before and after trauma, and d). Survivors could not recall meaningful academic school experiences.

Figure 3.3 Distributor: exploiter/trafficker.

lures, mixed with the personal economic crises many young women face, are contributing factors for young women being susceptible to sexual assault. All these opportunities for recruitment increase the vulnerability of girls to sexual assault throughout their childhood and adult lives.

Additionally, what makes young women most vulnerable to CSEC is that there is no one specific indicator that makes a girl vulnerable other than a lack of deep connection with family.

Foubert (2017), an expert on sexual violence against women in the 21st century, discusses the dangers of pornography and its impact on sexual violence toward women, especially among millennials. He states that over 88% of the scenes in pornographic footage display violence against a female by a male character. He also reports that generally, after the act of violence occurs toward the female by the male, the response by the female is either with sexual pleasure or no response at all. The most dangerous impact that this data has on children as young as eleven years old is that boys will be conditioned to believe "Girls like to be hit" and for girls, their response may be "If he hits me, maybe I should like it" (Foubert, 2017).

Survivor – Caregiver Relationship

Davies and Frawley (1994) discuss why a child's relationship with their caregiver is impacted by sexual trauma. Research shows that most children have been (sexually) abused and/or traumatized by their caregivers The relational view of sexual abuse trauma gives focus to the child attempting to regain positive connection with the abusive parent. The child's symptoms are based on an attempt to maintain the relationship with their caregiver (Davies & Frawley, 1994).

Most survivors live in a home with parents who come from families with insecure attachment relationships. Landreth (2012) and Moustaskas (1997) believe Relational Cultural Therapy (RCT) is a form of cognitive therapy which focuses on re-establishing positive relationships between child and caregiver must be utilized to orient a child's growth-fostering relationships (Landreth, 2012; Moustakas, 1997).

A child's response to their trauma relies heavily on their family's response to the trauma (Spaccarelli, 1994). Alexander (1992) proposes several types of family patterns that predict different outcomes. The three types of patterns in families are as follows: rejection pattern, role reversal/parentification pattern, and fear/unresolved trauma pattern (Alexander, 1992). Lenore Terr (1990) suggests that when childhood trauma survivors recall traumatic events in their environment, they can recreate painful memories (Terr, 1990).

Gil discusses the fact that children who have experienced trauma generally have had power and control exerted upon them (Gil, 2011). Jordan discusses sexual trauma as psychopathology. Jordan also explores RCT and its usefulness with child survivors of sexual abuse. "Experiencing mutuality and safety in relationships also produces shifts in the clients' inner experiences, self-statements, and self-image" (Jordan, 1991, p. 6).

It is important to incorporate and encourage healthy child-caregiver relationships where possible. Involving parents in strategizing for positive health outcomes for child survivors proves to be effective (Deblinger et al., 1996). Banks (2006) states that when children experience trauma, development may become stuck across multiple processes, including cognitive, psychosocial, moral, and relational development (Banks, 2006).

Trauma's impact on the brain is a crucial subcategory for me to explore because of the need to be informed on how a child's brain functions before strategizing on effective educational practices in schools.

Grooming

Based on current data available to researchers on the impact of sexual trauma on school experiences, it is necessary to explore the multiple intersectional aspects of childhood experiences to better understand the development of sexual trauma survivors even outside of school settings. Grooming is a concept that was first coined in 1886 (Dietz, 1983; Krafft-Ebbing, 1886) to center an understanding of how young children became at risk for sex trafficking and sexual exploitation. Since then, there have been additional contexts in which grooming lives must be examined in order to have a more holistic perspective of how the traumatized brain develops that may create challenges in making academic and social gains in school, which may in turn clarify the current gaps in current educational practice in supporting sexual trauma in schools. My hope is that in illuminating grooming culture, educators, educational leaders, and educational policymakers can begin to use this research to make more direct positively impactful decisions about how to re-think teaching and learning in educational settings for female sexual trauma survivors in school.

Research shows that there are systematic patterns in grooming behaviors by trusted adults toward child survivors that allow for victimization to have lasting impacts on the child and the caregiver-child relationship. According to Craven et al. (2006), there are currently various definitions on the definition of grooming for the purpose of sexual abuse of children. O'Connell (2003) defines grooming as "a course of conduct…that would give reason to believe… any meeting with the child would lead to conduct for unlawful purposes." Howitt (1995) described grooming as "steps taken to 'entrap' a victim (within a relationship)…analogous to adult courtship." van Dam (2002) defines grooming as "…a child is befriended…by…a would be abuser…in an attempt to gain the child's confidence…to acquiesce to abusive activity." Craven et al. (2006) acknowledge that both definitions reference the outdated term "pedophilia or pedophile." Not only that, but the term is often reserved within the context of a clinical diagnosis which may not include additional perpetrators of abuse. The term "pedophile" also contradicts more recent research that confirms most childhood sexual abuse occurs with a person that is familiar to the child, whereas "pedophile" implies detachment or disconnection from familiar ties to the child. Last, the above-cited terms contain subjective language that is left up to interpretation and heavily ridden with bias regarding what would be considered "substantial course of misconduct" or a "reasonable" individual identifying grooming behavior at the expense of the child. However, van Dam's (2002) definition is the most recent and conceptually appropriate for the current state of research in this field of study.

Craven et al. (2006) share the stages of the grooming process based on the current literature. This process may be used to center current understandings of grooming in various contexts familiar to girls who are at high risk for sexual trauma and abuse.

1 **Self-Grooming**: sexual offenders described this as a means of either justifying or denying their behavior having to do with cognitive distortions. Sexual offenders hold implicit theories regarding themselves and their relationship to potential victims as well as the world (Ward and Keenan (1999). Typically the offender's implicit theories may likely be considered

pathological, "maladaptive and supportive" of sex with children and have implications for their future behavior. The five justifications for sexual abuse of children by self-groomers are children as sexual objects, entitlement, dangerous world, uncontrollability, and nature of harm. The research is clear that based on sexual offender theory, children are at high risk for sexual trauma. However, for the sake of learning how to best support sexually traumatized girls in school, more understanding needs to be had regarding family systems and the environment and how both hold space for opportunities for sexual abuse of girls.

2 **Grooming the Environment and Significant Others:** begins with identifying vulnerability within the child. Typically, vulnerabilities are classified as harmed relationship with caregiver, lacking friends, and at least one previous incident of sexual abuse or misconduct. In this step of the process, the offender places themselves in environments that allow them the access of children (or women who are at high risk/have been victimized as children). This positions the offender as a person of trust in the environment. Offenders will groom the adults that are influential to the potential victim(s). Personality traits of groomers include charming, helpful, status, social capital, and so on. These personality traits are often utilized in positions of power and influence to create environments which breed opportunities for access to children for the offender. Offenders see access to children (and/or women) as their reward for their magnetic personality and work in their environment or community. According to Hare and Hart (1993), "Offenders are often able to read the community like a book" in that they assess what they need and fulfill their needs accordingly. They can make themselves indispensable, too good to be true and will freely undertake jobs that others do not want to do" (Leberg, 1997). Cognitive dissonance of caregivers often can aid in facilitating grooming, especially if the offender is an influential member of the community. The offender will often create a strong rapport with community members such that they become more believable than the victim if ever they were to disclose abuse within the community about the offender. This stage of grooming is detailed and organized intentionally. Intrafamilial child abuse research says that the offender specifically targets children who are raised by single parents, creating potential opportunity for fragmentation of adult caregiver implicit theory and allowing for easier access to the child because of a presumed need for additional role models in the child's life, especially creating justification for frequent alone time. Isolation from the child and their non-abusing parent typically and family members takes place in this stage of grooming as well. Isolation can also be orchestrated for the non-abusive parent or caregiver to either create distance from the abuse and/or to desensitize adults in the environment from the abuse while limiting interactions from future critics outside of the community environment. Offenders utilize explicit planning to draw vulnerable children into a

grooming relationship because of the low self-esteem and need for belonging that sexual offenders (of children) possess. They have a high sense of social cues from non-threatening children that offer a sense of accessibility and confidence that the offender may not feel with their peers.

3 **Grooming the Child:** according to the research, sexual offenders who are fathers in this stage, typically force their daughters to take the place of a romantic partner and may promote the child in place of the mother in intrafamilial abuse (Herman, 1981). Child grooming is typically classified under two categories: "physical grooming" and "psychological grooming."

Physical Grooming: it deals with increasing gradual sexualization of children with the offender. *Psychological grooming:* it refers to increased sexualization with the understanding that it is the job of the offender to teach or train the child on sexual health, or behavior with the justification of preparing the child for life later on (Berliner & Conte, 1990; Leberg, 1997). The strategy in this case is to build trust for a period of time and then to begin violating boundaries. The goal is to first interact with the child in non-threatening ways physically (handshake, touching the head, tickling, etc.) and gradually move toward inappropriate touching during engaging conversation to desensitize the child to inappropriate touch (Leberg, 1997).

Based on current research, while the term "grooming" is widely known and accepted, the diverse ways in which it is displayed in children are yet to be examined in the field. Most etiological theories of child sexual abuse neglect the phenomenon. Current research recommends that "it is necessary that theories be reconsidered based on this recent awareness" (Craven et al., 2006).

When examining survivor stories in this study, it became necessary to utilize current research with my study findings to add to the literature to support in creating explicit tools for female survivors of sexual trauma and to more easily identify risk factors. When it comes to intersectional understandings of sexual trauma according to survivor participants in the study, it became clear that there were social, cultural, racial, and even religious implications for risk factors for grooming and eventual sexual abuse of girls.

Below is a table that seeks to guide educators, educational leaders, and policymakers on considerations for psychological grooming and risk for sexual abuse of girls through the lens of intersectionality which are typically implicit and more challenging to identify an interrupt compared to physical grooming or actual assault. While this book seeks to examine opportunities for improvement of educational practices on behalf of survivors of sexual trauma, we must also acknowledge the communities and environments in which school-age girls are part of to better inform learning needs, behaviors, and socialization of girls who have experienced sexual trauma. The purpose of this table is to offer additional data points on how to potentially enhance and improve the school experiences of girls who have experienced sexual trauma.

Community/ environment	*Psychological grooming activities*
School communities	• Leveraging the power dynamic between the child and educator/ educational leader/school personnel. • Threatening negative academic outcomes for noncompliance with sexual misconduct or engagement. • Normalizing sexually charged conversation, coursework, comments, or behavior in the classroom and/or school with known lack of systems of accountability. • Sexualization of all, individuals, and/or groups of students (through dress, sex/gender, sexuality, and physical appearance). • Activities that promote, highlight, or normalize sexualization (of vulnerable and/or historically marginalized populations). • An environment that fosters explicit or implicit competition among students for the benefit of educators/educational leaders/ school personnel. • Expectations that go beyond the scope of "student" that are frequent, pervasive, and may/may not be documented.
Faith communities	• Individual and communal perceptions of faith leaders in religious spaces • Overuse of shame, guilt, sin-language to justify psychological and/or physical grooming • Weaponizing of passages from sacred texts to bring validity to grooming behavior • Explicit or implicit policing, organization of masses of women, children, populations in the areas of physical appearance, sexual conduct with peers, programming that lends itself to standardizing discussion, policies and procedures rooted in sex, sexual identity, or sexual preference. • Hyperfocus on personal or religious stances on sex, sexual identities, or ideologies. • Isolation from additional outside communities/individuals – even those who hold the same value systems • Gaslighting-setting norms that go against patterns of behavior or typical community practices • Explicit and implicit punitive and harsh punishments when expectations are not met • Expectations being facilitated, managed, and policed by another within the community/environment. • Explicit or implicit expectations of conduct based on gender (seating, behavior, dress, speech, and career choice) beyond family choice that is cultural and/or ties back to historical understandings of preference, culture, and/or sacred texts. • Psychological or physical servitude that is imbalanced or adds social capital to another and/or the faith leader. • Rewarding behavior that seeks the approval or affirmation of another • Scripted or pre-planned rejection or demotion that is meant to create competition for the attention and/or approval of another and/or faith leader. • Citing commitment to faith, family, culture, race, and/or community to justify grooming.

Community/ environment	*Psychological grooming activities*

Caregiver/ family (abusive or offending)	• Adultification
	    • Explicit or implicit comments or discussion on the physical appearance of the child.
	    • Deeming the child unworthy of or too old for care from an adult.
	    • Expecting independence and adult-level understanding, conduct, and behavior that goes beyond the child's developmental and social stage.
	• Parentification
	    • Explicit or implicit expectation of parenting (younger) siblings for the purpose of preparation for or resulting in sexual gratification of at least one parent, caregiver, or adult, which may be at the expense of the non-offending parent.
	• Introducing pornography and/or explicit adult content to desensitize sexual behavior
	• Isolation for the purpose of or resulting in sexual gratification of at least one parent, caregiver, or adult.
	• Leveraging cognitive dissonance of a non-offending caregiver for the purpose of or in preparation for sexual gratification of at least one offending parent, caregiver, or adult.
	• Normalizing unwanted physical touch
	• Establishing academic, developmental, or behavioral expectations of the child in an effort to create "people pleasing" in the child.
	• Citing faith, family, culture, race, and so on to justify grooming activities.

Workplace *Assuming the child is of legal working age and in workplace conditions that are suitable and legally acceptable.*	• Leveraging the power dynamic between the child and employer. • Threatening termination for noncompliance with sexual misconduct or engagement. • Normalizing sexually charged conversation or behavior in the workplace with known lack of systems of accountability. • Sexualization of groups of employees (through dress, sex/ gender, sexuality, and physical appearance). • Human resources protocols and procedures that are outdated, not enforced, or non-existent. • An environment that fosters explicit or implicit competition among colleagues for the benefit of the employer. • Expectations that go beyond the scope of work that are frequent, pervasive, and not documented in company documents, correspondence, or note-keeping documents. • Citing written or unwritten policies and procedures to justify grooming.

Survivors may experience some or all of the abovementioned descriptions of grooming. The impact of even one experience of grooming of a student survivor has a significant impact on student learning psychologically, socially, and academically. Additionally, when grooming is prolonged, the impact is of course more severe. An opportunity for research may be to conduct a comparative research study on the impact of psychological grooming with physical grooming on the educational experiences of student survivors of sexual trauma. In a subsequent study, it may be an effective addition to current research to examine whether or not psychological grooming survivor's academic needs present similarly as a survivor who has endured physical grooming and abuse.

References

ACE Awareness Foundation. (2014) Survey. Report: 52% of Shelby County Adults Experienced a Traumatic Event During Childhood. Available at: http://aceawareness.org/ace-survey/2014-survey. Accessed March 17, 2016.

Alexander, P. C. (1992). Application of attachment theory to the study of sexual abuse. *Journal of Consulting and Clinical Psychology*, *60*, 185–195.

Banks, A. (2006). Relational therapy for trauma. *Journal of Psychological Trauma*, *5*, 25–47. doi:10.1300/J189v05n01_03

Banks, D., & Kyckelhahn, T. (2011). Characteristics of Human Trafficking Incidents 2008–2010. U.S. Department of Justice: Official Justice Programs. https://www.ojp.gov/library/publications/characteristics-suspected-human-trafficking-incidents-2008-2010

Berliner, Lucy and Jon R. Conte. 1990. The process of victimization: the victims' perspective. *Child Abuse & Neglect 14*(1), 29–40. doi:10.1016/0145-2134(90)90078-8

Blodgett, C., & Dorado, J. (2016). A Selected Review of Trauma-Informed School Practice and Alignment with Educational Practice. http://ext100.wsu.edu/cafru/wpcontent/uploads/sites/65/2015/02/CLEAR-Trauma-Informed-Schools-White-Paper.pdf

Chafouleas, S.M., Johnson, J.H., Overstreet, S., & Santos, N.M., (2016). Toward a blueprint for trauma-informed service delivery in schools. *School Mental Health*, *8*, 144–162.

Chamberlain, P., Leve, L. D., & Smith, D. K. (2006). Preventing behavior problems and health risking behaviors. *International Journal of Behavioral Consultation and Therapy*, *2*(4). http://files.eric.ed.gov/fulltext/EJ804058.pdf

Coakely, M., & Lloyd, R. (2008). Human Trafficking: Commercial Sexual Exploitation of Children. CCIS Training Institute.

Cole, S. F., O'Brien, J. G., Gadd, M. G., Ristuccia, J., Wallace, D. L., & Gregory, M. (2005). *Helping traumatized children learn: Supportive school environments for children traumatized by family violence*. Massachusetts Advocates for Children.

Coster, W., & Cicchetti, D. (1993). Research on the communicative development of maltreated children: Clinical implications. *Topics in Language Disorders*, *13*, 25–38.

Craven, S., Brown, S., & Gilchrist, E. (2006). Sexual grooming of children: Review of literature and theoretical considerations. *Journal of Sexual Aggression*, *12*(3), 287–299. https://doi.org/10.1080/13552600601069414

Crenshaw, K. (1989). *Demarginalizing the intersection of race and sex: A black feminist critique of antidiscrimination doctrine, feminist theory and antiracist politics*. University of Chicago Legal Forum. Vol. 1989, Article 8. https://chicagounbound.uchicago.edu/uclf/vol1989/iss1/8

Crenshaw, K. & Peller, G. (1994). Reel Time/Real Justice, 70 Denv. U. L. Rev. 283.

Cronholm, P. F., Forke, C. M., Wade, R., Bair-Merritt, M. H., Davis, M., Harkins-Schwarz, M., Pachter, L. M., & Fein, J. A. (2015). Adverse childhood experiences: Expanding the concept of adversity. *American Journal of Preventive Medicine*, *49*(3), 354–361. https://doi.org/10.1016/j.amepre.2015.02.001

Davies, J. M., & Frawley, M. G. (1994). *Treating the adult survivor of childhood sexual abuse: A psychoanalytic perspective*. Basic Books.

Deblinger E, & Hemn A. H. (1996). *Treating sexually abused children and their nonoffending parents: A cognitive behavioral approach*. Thousand Oaks: Calif, Sage

Dietz, J. (1983). Theories of development. *Journal of Economic Issues*, *17*(4), 1160–1162. https://doi.org/10.1080/00213624.1983.11504203

Foa, E. B., Rothbaum, B. O., Riggs, D. S., & Murdock, T. B. (1991). Treatment of posttraumatic stress disorder in rape victims: A comparison between cognitive-behavioral procedures and counseling. *Journal of Consulting and Clinical Psychology*, *59*(5), 715–723. https://doi.org/10.1037/0022-006X.59.5.715

Foubert, J. D. (2017). The public health harms of pornography: The brain, erectile dysfunction, and sexual violence. *Dignity: A Journal on Sexual Exploitation and Violence*, *2*(3), 6. https://doi.org/10.23860/dignity.2017.02.03.06. Available at: http://digitalcommons.uri.edu/dignity/vol2/iss3/6

Gill, C. J., Sander, A. M., Robins, N., Mazzei, D. K., & Struchen, M. A. (2011). Exploring experiences of intimacy from the viewpoint of individuals with traumatic brain injury and their partners. *The Journal of head trauma rehabilitation*, *26*(1), 56–68. https://doi.org/10.1097/HTR.0b013e3182048ee9

Hare, R. D., & Hart, S. D. (1993). Psychopathy, mental disorder, and crime. In S. Hodgins (Ed.), *Mental disorder and crime* (pp. 104–115). Sage Publications, Inc.

Helge, D. (1992, March). Child Sexual Abuse in America: A Call for School & Community Action. A Report of a National Study. *Western Washington University. Bellingham National Rural Development Institute*. http://files.eric.ed.gov/fulltext/ED345141.pdf

Herman, J. L. (1981). Father-Daughter Incest, Harvard University Press, Cambridge, Mass

Hill Collins, P. (2000). *Black feminist thought: Knowledge, consciousness, and the politics of empowerment* (2nd ed.). Routledge Press.

Howitt, D. (1995). *Paedophiles and sexual offences against children*. John Wiley & Sons.

Jordan, J. (1991). Empathy, mutuality, and therapeutic change: Clinical implications of a relational model. In J. V. Jordan, A. G. Kaplan, J. B. Miller, I. P. Stiver, & J. L. Surrey (Eds.), *Women's growth in connection: Writings from the Stone Center* (pp. 283–289). New York, NY: Guilford.

Kilpatrick, D. Saunders, B. & Smith, W. (2003). Youth Victimization: Prevalence and Implications. *U.S. Department of Justice Office of Justice Programs*. https://www.ncjrs.gov/pdffiles1/nij/194972.pdf

King, E. H. (1983). Assessment and Treatment of Sexually Abused Children and Adolescents. Symposium Papers Presented at the American Psychological Association. http://files.eric.ed.gov/fulltext/ED241851.pdf

Krafft-Ebing, R. (1886). *Psychopathia sexualis*. Reprinted by Bloat Books. ISBN 0-9650324-1-8

Landreth, G. (2012). *Play therapy: The art of the relationship* (3rd ed.). Routledge-Taylor & Francis.

Leberg, E. (1997). *Understanding child molesters: Taking charge*. Thousand Oaks, CA: SAGE.

Lee, B., & Newberg, A. (2005). *Neuroimaging in Traumatic Brain Imaging, 2*(2), 372–83. http://dx.doi.org/10.1602/neurorx.2.2.372

Morris, A. M., Mrug, S. & Windle, M. (2015). From family violence to dating violence: Testing a dual pathway model. *J Youth Adolescence 44*, 1819–1835. https://doi.org/10.1007/s10964-015-0328-7

Moustakas, C. (1997). *Relationship play therapy*. Northvale, NJ: Aronson.

National Center for Missing & Exploited Children (2022). *Office of Juvenile Delinquency Prevention.* 2002 Annual Report. https://www.missingkids.org/footer/about/annual-report

O'Connell, R. (2003). A Typology of Cyber Sexploitation and Online Grooming Practices. Preston: University of Central Lancashire. http://image.guardian.co.uk/sys-files/Society/documents/2003/07/24/Netpaedoreport.pdf

Scheeringa, M. S., Weems, C. F., Cohen, J. A., Amaya-Jackson, L., & Guthrie, D. (2011). Trauma-focused cognitive-behavioral therapy for posttraumatic stress disorder in three-through six year-old children: A randomized clinical trial. *Journal of Child Psychology and Psychiatry, and Allied Disciplines, 52*(8), 853–860. https://doi.org/10.1111/j.1469-7610.2010.02354.x

Skiba, R. J., Artiles, A. J., Kozleski, E. B., Losen, D. J., & Harry, E. G. (2016). Risks and consequences of oversimplifying educational inequities: A response to Morgan et al. (2015). *Educational Researcher, 45*(3), 221–225. https://10.3102/0013189X16644606

Spaccarelli, S. (1994). Stress, appraisal, and coping in child sexual abuse: a theoretical and empirical review. *Psychological Bulletin, 116* (2), 340–362.

Terr, L. (1990). *Too scared to cry: Psychic trauma in childhood.* Harper & Row Publishers.

Truman, J. L., & Langton, L., (2014). Criminal victimization. *Bureau of Justice Statistics*. https://www.bjs.gov/content/pub/pdf/cv14.pdf

Toomey, A., Brennan, E. M., & Friesen, B. (2008). Resilience theory as a framework for teaching human development within HBSE. Retrieved from http://www.rtc.pdx.edu/PDF/pbResilienceTheory.pdf

Townsend, C., & Rheingold, A. A. (2013). Estimating a child sexual abuse prevalence rate for practitioners: A review of child sexual abuse prevalence studies. *Darkness to Light*. www.D2L.org/1in10

Walby, S., Armstrong, J., & Strid, S. (2012). Intersectionality: Multiple inequalities in social theory. *Sociology, 46*(2), 224–240. https://doi.org/10.1177/0038038511416164

Ward, T., & Keenan, T. (1999). Child Molesters' implicit theories. *Journal of Interpersonal Violence, 14*(8), 821–838. https://doi.org/10.1177/088626099014008003

Williams, W., Karlin, T., & Wallace, D. (2012). Project SisterCircle: Risk, intersectionality and intervening in urban schools. *Journal of School Counseling*. http://files.eric.ed.gov/fulltext/EJ981197.pdf

4 The Psychological Impact of Sexual Trauma

Survivor Stories

According to survivor responses, there is a psychological impact of sexual trauma. The psychological impact of trauma results in challenges with identity and belonging in school. The psychological impact includes psychological disruption, developmental delays and challenges, and inability to navigate relationships, especially relationships with caregivers and identity. The following is a series of survivor reports that reveal the psychological impact of sexual trauma as well as current research that discusses the need to address trauma from a psychological perspective for survivors.

Very social because it was a cover up, but was not sexually active. I was in the Art honors society, and enjoyed being around people because it never made me feel alone, but I had a lot of abandonment and attachment issues. I put myself through a lot of stress. I now deal with Chronic PTSD, Borderline Personality Disorder, and anxiety/depression. Everyday this is a battle but everyday this makes me stronger.

I was an overall B student. I was relatively quiet in class. I did my assignments in school and had little homework. I skipped some classes in high school but not full days. I was never called on it. During my sophomore year, I frequently told my mom I didn't want to go to school. For one semester, I missed about a day a week.

I didn't think I would look out the window at the birds for hours so I didn't learn.

I had two traumatic experiences within a year of each other. The first was losing my mother and later that year on a trip overseas, I was molested by neighbors. I was 6 years old. I was in second grade. I was very shy and quiet, uncomfortable around men.

My teacher had us write letters to our deceased loved ones. Everything occurred after my family member passed away. When the teacher asked why I was crying I told her I missed my family member which I did, but I was hurting more because I was being raped and no one knew.

DOI: 10.4324/9781032648668-5

My first recall or memory was when I was first arrested, before 6 or 7. (247) First arrest was shoplifting. Three ties at 18, twice at 19. At 21 it was my 6th or 7th time. And I learned from those experiences and I'm able to talk about it because of those experiences. The reason I felt like I made those decisions, I was lost, I was angry at myself and others. I never had a good relationship with my family, especially my mom.

I remember sitting in Child Development class in high school and learning about childhood sexual abuse and thinking, wow, that's what happened to me. I think that was the first time I realized what happened to me. It was both a relief and a shock. I didn't tell anyone when I was a young child and I didn't tell anyone then, but I do remember writing for each answer on a test in a different class, "why me?" The trauma happened to me before Kindergarten so it really happened to me so early that it followed me throughout my life and my schooling.

My traumatic experiences started as young as I can remember and didn't end until I was ten. Two instances occurred after I was ten with another person. So there really wasn't any sense of before and after for me. All of my experiences were colored with trauma. The trauma happened so early I think it became the norm as far as my behavior in school and concerns with that. I remember being tired in the mornings from being up at night.

The abuse started before I entered school and lasted until I was a teenager.

Gender plays a role. There's a long time where people didn't believe me, they would accuse me of lying, attention seeking or being over dramatic. You're being sensitive. You're looking for something to be wrong with you so people will pay attention to you. You don't have a lot of friends so maybe you're doing this to gain sympathy and friends. So for me to be a girl who is dealing with sexual trauma means to not be believed and to be dismissed and overlooked.

My identity doesn't come into play with my sexual trauma because I didn't have one. I couldn't tell you. I never had a favorite meal or a favorite thing. I had nothing specific that would identify or differentiate me from anyone else. I just exist.

In my culture and as a woman with the experience of sexual trauma, we don't tend to share our experiences, especially with school officials. We're taught not to talk about it. So it didn't go as far as telling a teacher or anything. I just went to school, and dealt with my thoughts, and psychological issues silently. He only made me hate myself even more and made the people around me hate me as well. Or at least I thought they all hated me. I did not bother to let anyone know what happened to me because I felt like it was just another hiccup in my life since things like that have been happening to me since I was in elementary school.

There were teachers who tried to touch me before and after class when no one was around. He did it when no one was around to see anything. But only he and I knew what was happening. The athletic coaches made me feel uncomfortable too. I would be walking up and down the hallways, into classrooms, and empty offices, looking for people and I just felt hands groping me all day long. I would go home and take hot showers just to feel clean again. Then go to school and get groped all day all over again. I wondered how no one saw it. In all the years that I was in school, how did no one notice the groping–ever? I never told on them I just never let myself be alone with them.

The survivor response data analyzed for guiding research question one had to do with how participants reported their interaction with the individuals in their schools and how those interactions impacted their psychological development. According to the research, sexual trauma can be isolating in nature. The purpose of this aspect of the data analysis was to examine how participants perceived their ability to be successful in school psychologically based on their individual interactions in school. In the analysis of data that sought to answer guiding research question one, I wondered how individual interactions confirmed or disproved what the literature says about the psychological impact of sexual trauma.

Data Collected and Analyzed for Guiding Research Questions One and Two

The categories that emerged from the first guiding question and the theme of the psychological impact of sexual trauma are as follows: (a) survivors reported feeling invisible in school, (b) survivors reported feeling lost in school, (c) survivors reported internal struggles, and (d) survivors reported ambivalence about their identities.

Survivors Reported Feeling Invisible in School

Many survivors reported feeling invisible in school. They experienced challenges with finding their niche in school. Lavender, age 61, stated that her family did not respond to her revelation of her own sexual abuse and trauma. She shared:

I remember sitting in Child Development class in high school and learning about childhood sexual abuse and thinking, wow, that's what happened to me. I think that was the first time I realized what happened to me. No one said or did a thing. If my parents were contacted, they didn't say anything to me. The teacher didn't say anything to me. I felt like it was a confirmation that no one saw me or heard me (June 17, 2020).

This memory suggests that Lavender, like many other survivors, had a revelation of their trauma and how it is so closely intertwined with their development, their identity, and their perspective in the world. The memory illustrates the strong impact of trauma, particularly because the first area that is impacted is one's psychological development. In addition to how trauma impacts psychological development, it also impacts survivor identity, particularly around race, class, and gender.

Marigold, age 33, recalled that her family's socioeconomic status made her feel less visible in school.

> I think that being poor made me less visible, and I had started to internalize my discomfort with my family's socioeconomic status right around the time I experienced the initial trauma. I started to feel more intolerant of authority which changed how others perceived me in school…which increased my feelings of shame and of being unwelcome and unsafe at school.
>
> (Interview, June 19, 2020)

Iris, age 48, described her experience of isolation in her statement.

> All I wanted was to be invisible and as a fat kid that was impossible. I was picked on all the time, never had a boyfriend. I was not invited to events and spent all my time trying to hide. I never raised my hand to ask questions or answer questions.
>
> (Interview, June 20, 2020)

Although more literature discusses how to support children who have been sexually abused, since the 1980s, that literature remains fragmented (Leve & Smith, 2006; McNally et al., 2022; Miragoli et al., 2017) and calls for standardization of intervention and prevention programs (especially in schools). Lately, more literature supports and justifies the need for specialized programming; however, that literature does not yet provide systematic advice for collecting the kind of best practices that would help develop a program based on the available literature and self-reports by young women.

Survivors Reported Feeling Lost in School

Survivors also reported feeling lost or unable to engage in school as a result of their sexual trauma. Based on the guiding questions, it was really important to me that as the researcher I kept in mind how the lived experiences of survivors impacted how educators and school leaders practice trauma sensitivity in school. The following discussion describes how survivors described the feelings of being lost and unable to engage in school as a result of the psychological impact of sexual trauma.

Forsythia stated: "I had a lot of abandonment and attachment issues. I put myself through a lot of stress. I now deal with Chronic PTSD, Borderline Personality Disorder, and anxiety/depression. Everyday this is a battle" (Interview, June 22, 2020). Lavender discussed:

> I skipped some classes in high school…I was never called on it. I frequently told my mom I didn't want to go to school. For one semester,

> I missed about a day a week. My excuse to mom was I didn't want to go, I wanted to stay at home.
>
> (Interview, June 25, 2020)

Nerine, age 30, described feeling like she was walking on eggshells in her high school relationship. She stated:

> I dated someone that was emotionally and physically abusive. He put his hands around my neck when he was upset with me…He often threatened to kill himself as a way of controlling me. He also pinched my arms and left marks on my arms.
>
> (Interview, June 14, 2020)

In general, survivors who experience intimate partner violence are likely to be isolated from friends and family or anyone who will challenge the normalcy of the abuse. Unfortunately, this reality is intensified for girls in school who have experienced sexual assault. Many times, girls inevitably choose to wrestle with this challenge alone fearing the consequences of being vocal about the abuse or seeking general support.

Survivors Reported Internal Struggles

Additionally, a subcategory that emerged from survivor data revealed that survivors reported how the psychological impact of trauma caused an internal struggle. The internal struggle that survivors discussed typically had to do with self-acceptance around physical size, race, gender, class, or socioeconomic status. The struggle that survivors identified exacerbated their response to the trauma as well as negatively impacted their overall self-concept.

When asked *"what kind of a school do you go to?"* – a more broad question that typically causes the participant to think about the school environment, culture, and climate most answered with the divisions between classes, races, and socioeconomic status. They reported recalling who had money and who didn't. They even reported the perception of members of the school community and of how cliques and subgroups were formed. For example, Rosemary, age 31, a White woman, age 31, discussed her perception of the groups of friends she spent time with in school. She described her friend group as out of the ordinary because, in the middle of her school career, three districts combined three demographics of the student population to create one larger school for the community. Because of the combining of districts, the two codes of feeling alone as well as division of classes and status were both in play in this particular participant experience. She continued by describing the drastic difference between affluent students and students who are living in poverty. "I attended a predominantly White and wealthy town in a class of about 100 students and the other a private

Christian school with about 13 people in my class with moderate to low diversity" (Interview June 16, 2020).

Amaryllis, Latina, age 26, reported the inability to focus on school because of feeling like she was not represented or seen in a suburban school community. She reported attending a predominantly White exam school for middle and high school.

> My race, my societal status impacted how people treated me and I was looked at because I was promiscuous. People always knew I dated guys outside of school and they were older guys, so it was always like 'ew.' So I think that impacted me because I wanted to have power somehow.
>
> (Interview, June 9, 2020)

Additionally, Cora, age 45, discussed her parent's desire to change schools to the White suburban school district with the understanding that she would receive a quality education. "Middle School Upper middle class-Blacks were bussed to the school…I was moved there to get help with my reading…" (Interview, June 10, 2020). Azalea, age 33, shared:

> I didn't have as much money as people in the public school community. If you didn't have a house or the ability to go on certain vacations. Feeling excluded because people assumed you didn't want to go when really, you couldn't afford to go.
>
> (Interview, June 10, 2020)

Magnolia, age 56 shared:

> My family values and socio-economic standing had a huge impact on my experiences as a sexual trauma survivor at school. We were a blended family with no money. There was a lot of dysfunction being modeled and because I spent most of my time playing school and community sports, I didn't really get that all families didn't run like ours.
>
> (Interview, June 19, 2020)

Survivors Reported Ambivalence About Their Identities

Survivors also discussed the intensity of the psychological impact of sexual trauma by discussing the fact that their trauma occurred at such a young age, that it seemed that the trauma presented a disruption in their identity and formed their identity itself. So, they learned to grow and develop with the impact of trauma alongside them since the time that their traumatic event occurred. Lavender, age 61, presented her perspective on how her trauma impacted her identity. She stated feeling that because of the trauma, she did not know who she was and she often struggled with trying to understand herself.

Many of the participants who reported trauma at a young age did not have distinguishing points in their childhood that they could identify when the trauma shifted their attitude about who they were individually. They grew into their trauma as they grew into themselves simultaneously.

The realization of how trauma impacts identity forms how survivors navigate school. Amaryllis, age 26, reported:

> I didn't have the choice to have an identity. I was always on the defense. Because of trying to always protect myself I was the offender. After a while I had to make sure I had control over certain situations. Being a woman, being Hispanic, all of that works against you.

Survivors understanding the need to examine their identity simultaneously with their trauma highlights the theory of intersectionality and the reality that it exists within the lived experience of sexual trauma survivors.

The following describes categories detailing participant recollections of how the psychological impact of trauma influenced their identity.

> I remember a time sitting on the couch at home and wondering why I was so different, why I didn't fit in…I always felt like a fraud, like I was pretending to be me, because I had no idea who I was. I didn't know me and no one else knew me…I thought everyone was like me but were better fakers than I was….
>
> (Interview, June 17, 2020)

Survivor lived experiences uncover the reality that exists when navigating school post-trauma. The reality is that survivors often feel like they have lost themselves or are not in touch with who they truly are. It seems that their identity post-trauma is being established for them (because of the psychological impact of trauma) rather than having the opportunity to explore their identity as an individual who has not experienced trauma. Also, oftentimes, the psychological impact of trauma can cause survivors to make choices or behave in ways that are out of their control. Forsythia, age 22, shared that she learned how quickly her assault resulted in deviant behavior but also how her status in her family was lowered because of the perception of her and why she was acting out.

> I was lost, I was angry at myself and others. That's not the image I want to portray because I was 'privileged.' Now I'm the black sheep. I got probation. I got arrested again on probation and that was my last arrest. I was made fun of a lot for being overweight…when I got into high school my freshman year, I (15 years old at the time) was raped by a junior at a small get together. I was pretty lost…I ran from my issues. I always wanted to be the center of attention, but by eleventh grade I would officially say I lost myself truly.
>
> (Interview, June 16, 2020)

It was when survivors were asked the question *As you recall your time in school. What are some experiences that come to mind that can help me understand what school was like for you as a student?* The data began to shift from a focus on loneliness and power dynamics to an additional theme of acknowledgment of gender dynamics. Additionally, here begins a clear example of intersectionality and how the multiple identities of the survivors which in this case include being female, being sexual trauma survivors, and being students all come into play. The sexism here in the case of survivor reports does not necessarily have anything to do with what one would typically think of when they hear sexism such as equal pay. Because survivors are reporting from a place of being youth it was imperative that I be intentional about recognizing moments where intersectionality was at play without getting consumed with the adult perspective of how intersectionality shows up based on my studies and professional experiences.

Intersectionality plays a role in female students around sexual assault. Intersectionality was present in the stories and lived experiences of the survivors such as survivors seeking support through disclosure and confronting their abusers. One survivor in particular reported at a young age understanding the level of influence that a male perpetrator can have in creating a system that is unwilling to hear of any wrongdoing by affluent males that are generally perceived as outgoing, popular, funny, and charismatic. Survivors mostly discussed how they perceived their gender, race, or socioeconomic background contributed to how they navigated school given their experience with sexual trauma. While participants recognized that the ways they identify inform their experience, they mostly reflected about the trauma itself and how it shaped their thinking about their sexuality, status, and power while they were students. Similarly, Cora, age 45, shared:

> Being aware that women are more susceptible to traumatic experiences or people taking advantage of women. I never–you know how you had girls who hang out with a lot of guys. I never did that. All my encounters with friends were female friends. So cross gender socialization was impacted.
>
> (Interview, June 15, 2020)

Forsythia, age 23, discussed:

> I did not date or become sexual for about 2 years after my experience. I had a wall up for emotions to everybody for about 8 years and trust in general is still not there. I still feel like I walk on eggshells.
>
> (Interview, June 13. 2020)

Participants also reported feelings of safety in school as they relate to gender. Anise, age 34, disclosed: "In high school some teachers (males were a little too close to the female students.) So, I stayed away from those teachers. I never became comfortable around male teachers" (Interview, June 13, 2020).

When asked about psychological, social, and academic experiences in school, survivor responses were grouped into the following three categories: (a) survivors reported remedies for psychological impact of sexual trauma in school; (b) survivors reported remedies for social impact of sexual trauma in school; and (c) survivors remedies for academic impact of sexual trauma in school.

Survivors report psychological impact of sexual trauma. Based on the themes that emerged from survivor responses, the results reflect the complexity of trauma based on the various areas in student learning that it impacts. Based on survivor responses to the lived experience in school, we see that the traumatic event impacted the survivor's psychological development. In accordance with the academic literature, there is a clear correlation between the experience of trauma and its psychological impact. Participant responses highlight this reality based on their first-hand accounts of their self-perception in school and how they navigated school post-trauma.

- To answer the question, "What systems, factors, and conditions, if any, do survivors recall as most supportive in middle and high school?" The following interview questions were asked of participants to answer guiding research question two:
- How did your (identifier) intersect and impact your experience as a sexual trauma survivor in school?
- How did your identity as a woman intersect and impact your social/racial experience as a sexual trauma survivor in school?
- As you recall your school experiences after the traumatic experience, what are some things that were said or done by people at your school that you found helpful?
- As you recall that time in your life after your traumatic experience, what are some things you wish people at school had said or had done that you now think would have helped?
- As you recall your school experience, what are some ways that people at school attempted to be helpful but you wished they did not try?

According to Simon and Cathy (1993), sexual assault among high school young people is at epidemic proportions. Many schools have protocols to address disclosures based on their state laws but often refer sexually assaulted young women to the Department of Children and Families from a fear or hesitation to get involved. Obviously, because sexual assault is so ubiquitous, schools must be more intentional about providing safe spaces for disclosures. State laws for sexual assault differ from the laws that *protect* children from sexual assault (Simon & Cathy, 1993). Inconsistencies in how the law protects and reports circumstances of sexual assault among girls can significantly impact them psychologically which inevitably will impact their success in school.

Neuroendocrine regulates moods, stress responses, the immune system, and digestive disruption. Once trauma is a factor, the abused child is more likely than the healthy child to develop psychological and physiological problems. After trauma occurs, there is a decrease in hippocampal volume which is responsible for special awareness, memories, and events. This part of the brain also facilitates making sense of incoming information and responds to stress. With chronic trauma, the hippocampus begins to atrophy and to lose its function abilities (Rothschild, 2004).

Eventually, the ultimate danger of trauma and its impact on the brain is that it leads to depression, suicide, or other at-risk behaviors that are harmful to the child. Chen et al. (2009) describe the protein molecule called NR3CI which is typically found in the central nervous system (CNS) of individuals experiencing high levels of psychological stress and post-traumatic stress disorder. This protein molecule impacts the hippocampus which when met with high levels of stress from trauma can lead to anxiety, depression, and suicide. Cozolino (2010) emphasizes that even in the womb, the fetus understands trauma and communicates a stress response to trauma. From birth, the child is constantly anticipating stress or the trauma to reoccur. This leads to higher levels of cortisol and eventually higher likelihood of depression in adulthood (Cozolino, 2010; Gunnar, 1998).

References

Chamberlain, P., Leve, L. D., & Smith, D. K. (2006). Preventing Behavior Problems and Health Risking Behaviors in. International Journal of Behavioral Consultation and Therapy, *2*(4). http://files.eric.ed.gov/fulltext/EJ804058.pdf

Chen, Y., Smith, D., & Meaney, D. (2009). In-vitro approaches for studying blast-induced traumatic brain injury. *Journal of Neurotrauma, 26*(6), 861–876. http://doi.org/10.1089/neu.2008.0645

Cozolino, L. (2010). *The neuroscience of psychotherapy* (2nd ed.). Norton.

Gunnar, M. (1998). Quality of early care and buffering of neuroendocrine stress reactions: Potential effects on the developing human brain. *Journal of Preventive Medicine*, *27*(2), 208–211.

Jones, P. J., & McNally, R. J. (2022). Does broadening one's concept of trauma undermine resilience? *Psychological Trauma: Theory, Research, Practice, and Policy, 14*(S1), S131–S139. https://doi.org/10.1037/tra0001063

Miragoli, S., Camisasca, E., & Di Blasio, P. (2017). Child Sexual Behaviors in School Context: Age and Gender Differences. *Journal of Child Sexual Abuse*, *26*(2), 213–231. https://doi.org/10.1080/10538712.2017.1280866

Rothschild, B. (2004). Applying the brakes. *Psychotherapy Networker*, *28*(1).

Rothschild, B. (2004b). Mirror mirror: Emotion in the consulting room is more contagious than we thought. *Psychotherapy Networker*, *28*(5), 46–50.

Simon, T. B., & Cathy, H. A. (1993). Sex Without Consent. Volume I: Peer Education Training for Secondary Schools. Learning Publications, Inc., 1. http://files.eric.ed.gov/fulltext/ED378505.pdf

5 The Social Impact of Sexual Trauma

Meet Rose

At the public schools I was very studious and athletic and very antisocial, I would sit with others and socialize if need be but essentially felt 100% alone with no actual friend to call me real friend within my grade, this is the same for my public high school minus the sports. At the private schools, middle and high, I was very open, very social and could mostly consider every student a friend of mine. I didn't do much socially, I wasn't involved in any clubs or sports. I have tears in my eyes as I say this, due in part to the overall stress of the pandemic, but also because my heart aches for my younger self. I remember a time sitting on the couch at home and wondering why I was so different, why I didn't fit in, why it was so difficult to hold onto the feeling of peace and safety that I so seldom felt. I always felt like a fraud, like I was pretending to be me, because I had no idea who I was. I didn't know me and no one else knew me. I was sad but didn't know it. I thought everyone was like me but were better fakers than I was. I wanted to be invisible and I attempted to be all the time. I had one friend, but I never told anyone about the abuse after I told the guidance counselor.

Rose didn't really want many friends. She didn't trust crowds of people. Rose was very athletic. She participated in almost every sport because she didn't like to go home. Rose was a good student who earned good grades and was a teacher-pleaser, until her grade 12 year where drinking and partying got in the way. Rose began skipping out to party or to nurse a hangover. She was always the life of the party–Rose partied a lot. Lots of drinking to black out and sleeping around. She tried drugs a tiny bit. By grade 11, it wasn't until after her first marriage dissolved that she dabbled a bit more in that area of partying hard. For Rose, the poison was drinking and sex. She felt excluded and continued to have trust issues. Everyone was really close because they went to school and grew up together. Rose reports that she could have done better as a student. However, she felt like her grades didn't matter.

Rose remembers in 2nd grade struggling with reading and at that time, her mother switched her out of that school into another school where it was

DOI: 10.4324/9781032648668-6

predominantly white middle and upper class and that's when the school system started bussing students. Rose didn't feel the need to challenge herself because no one really challenged her. Rose ran away from home as soon as she legally could.

Meet Diamond

Teachers were confused always asking "why are you acting like this?" Diamond's mother was called a lot. Diamond was hurting. Diamond felt misunderstood often. She was withdrawn. Diamond was quiet after the abuse incident happened to her. She was lashing out. She had a fascination with sex. During her teenage years, Diamond's hormones were out of whack. She wanted a boyfriend not to have a companion but because she wanted to have sex. But, maybe, according to Diamond "curious" is a better word. Diamond reported that her feelings were due to her trauma happening at such a young age. In fourth grade, her teacher had her peers write letters to their deceased loved ones. Diamond's assault occurred after her grandmother passed away. She remembers writing letters to her and crying in class. When the teacher asked why Diamond was crying, Diamond told her "I miss my Nana," when yes she missed her grandmother, however, she was hurting more because she was being manipulated into allowing rape. Diamond's abuser liked the school bus driver. Her abuser told her that if she convinced the bus driver to date him, he would not hurt her again.

Diamond remembers sitting in Child Development class in high school and learning about childhood sexual abuse and thinking, the same happened to her. It was the first time Diamond realized what happened to her. It was both a relief and a shock. She didn't tell anyone when she was a young child and didn't tell anyone then.

Meet April

April reported feeling like she was just a face. She stated that she was not known and not popular but also not an outcast. She was in the middle. Not hated but at the same time not loved. She was just on the outskirts. High school was the same. Eventually she became less? She was not as withdrawn. She moved around a lot and in her hometown, all the kids grew up together so it took her some time for people to get to know her and she had to struggle to find her friend group. At the public schools, April was very studious, athletic and very antisocial. She would sit with others and socialize if need be but essentially felt 100% alone with no actual friend to call her real friends within her grade, this is the same for public high school.

April always felt like her knowledge of things was deeper than other students, she felt like her opinions were shaped by a 30 year old not a naive 12 or 13 year old. Some of her peers were fairly naive to this day being ignorant to the workings of different social classes and the inability to even believe that anyone ever had hardships. She would hide a lot. She was constantly being found in another room off of the floor that she was actually supposed to be on. So when counselors or the principals would come looking for her, she was always there but it was never where her classes were- it was always somewhere else. She felt lost.

April dropped out when she was in junior high and tried to go back a few times without successfully re-engaging. She had a lot of social anxiety in school and felt like her peers looked down on her. She went mostly unnoticed by adults in the school, even when she would get up and leave the school in the middle of class. They tended to be very surprised when she would show up for tests and get high scores without having attended class or done homework. She did get in trouble a bit when she tried to go to the regular high school because she would sneak out and smoke cigarettes and joints with her friends off campus during the day.

Data Collected and Analyzed for Guiding Research Question Two

The data analyzed for guiding research question two had to do with how participants reported their interaction with their school systems. In comparison to the data analyzed to answer guiding research question one (which examined participant interactions with individuals in school), the data analyzed in research question two had more to do with how participants interacted with their schools as systems. The data analysis for guiding research question two sought to understand how the interactions between participants and school systems impacted their social experiences in school post-trauma. Within the theme of social impact as a result of sexual trauma exist three categories: a) survivors reported feeling isolated in school, b) survivors did not have meaningful connections with family or friends, c) survivors reported being labeled as deviant and felt misunderstood, and d) survivors reported feeling silenced in school.

Survivors Reported Isolation in School

When it comes to the school experiences of sexual trauma survivors, one of the most reported feelings by participants in the study was isolation. In the first category, participants used the words "lonely," "left out," or "by myself" to describe their experiences as students. These codes represent the fact that all participants regardless of their cultural background, age and economic status reported feelings of loneliness and isolation as a result of their experience of sexual trauma. Finkelhor (1978) defined sexual victimization and reported the widespread sexual abuse of children. Finkelhor surveyed 795 college undergraduates about their childhood sexual experiences. In Finkelhor's sample, 19% of females and 9% of males experienced sexual abuse with most victimization occurring in the child's family home. Finkelhor also found that, although sexual abuse cuts across social and economic lines, it was more prevalent among families of lower class or rural backgrounds where abusers took advantage of the victim's isolation. Finkelhor also found that many sexual experiences go unreported. It is important to recognize that based on the current body of research, girls in marginalized communities are most likely to be sexually assaulted as well as not report the assault. Daisy, age 31, reported that she felt unwanted and unseen in school stating that: "I was just a face. Not known, not popular and not an outcast" (Interview. June 13, 2020). While Amaryllis, age 26, recalls her school experiences: "I didn't have any friends," and another, Azalea, age 33, reported "[being] Alone…no friends…utterly alone and unheard" (Interview. June 11, 2020).

In a final example, Forsythia, age 23, described being teased for being overweight and being assaulted repeatedly in high school. The impact of the assaults exacerbated the challenges she was already experiencing being a survivor of sexual assault. Rosemary, age 31, described that even after having found a diverse friend group, feeling isolated from her White peers because it was not socially acceptable to be friends with non-whites in her community. She states: "Our high school was 99% white. We had very little of any other demographic…I remember being stared at when I hung out with my friends who were not White. But the White students didn't include me so I'm not sure what they expected me to do?…Middle school people thought we were snooty so I didn't have a lot of friends in 6th and 7th grade, I was bullied really bad. I loved it but I left basketball because of [the bullies]" (Interview. June 9, 2020).

The majority of participants reported feeling a sense of loneliness and isolation as their primary experience as sexual trauma survivors in school. Despite having friend groups or connectedness at home, based on participant reports, there is an intangible, inevitable feeling of loneliness in school after having experienced childhood sexual trauma.

Survivors experienced having no friends or lacking a connection with family members

Because of the social impact of sexual trauma, many participants reported challenges with making meaningful connections with friends and family. Nerine, age 30, shared her experience with struggling to make connections: "Academically I was fine. I took advanced classes in everything but math. I was rebellious and super explosive. Socially I also lost friends which hurt… senior year was horrible" (Interview. June 20, 2020). Primrose, age 29, echoes this experience by sharing that she recalled not even wanting close friendships or relationships and not understanding why. She stated: "I remember not having friends wanting to make friends. I thought it was because I was an only child, I was really awkward. With my teachers I got along with my teachers. There's always that weird male teacher that you thought was a creep. I knew creeps because I knew from what I went through. I just wanted girlfriends, but boys wanted sexual activities" (Interview. June 15, 2020).

Another participant reported that being an African American woman, it was not always culturally acceptable to disclose abuse and to invite school officials into the home and personal experiences. She recalls that from a young girl, she was positioned as unable to trust authorities after her assault. She had to proceed with caution ensuring that she did not further open herself up to further mistrust and scrutiny from authorities outside the home (Cora, age 45, June 15, 2020).

Magnolia, age 56, discussed the consequence she received for disclosing her abuse. "I had suffered abuse from a…member of the family. This abuse I felt I could talk about. I told a friend at school. And I told my parents. In the end, I got in trouble for telling. The friend I told never told anyone…and the topic was never spoke of again" (June 21, 2020).

One of the most common experiences of survivors is gaslighting. Sarkis (2017) defines gaslighting as a tactic that makes victims second guess themselves and their reality. Some examples of gaslighting include lying, denial, and convincing the community that the victim is lying. Unfortunately, survivors in this study reported feeling many forms of gaslighting with the intent of keeping them silent about the abuse. Rosemary, age 31, discussed the impact of trauma in relation to gender relations. She stated: "Gender plays a role. There's a long time where people didn't believe me, they wouldn't believe me, they would accuse me of lying, attention seeking or being over dramatic. His dad was one of the teachers in my school. He was the economics teacher. His dad was on wall street as a broker. They were wealthy. For a 16-year-old boy to drive a huge SUV wasn't typical. He was popular and his house was huge. He had money to have the parties. He had money to supply alcohol and weed. Unheard of in our area and our school. So, when I told people it was like you're trying to drag him down he's so cool." She also experienced name-calling, gaslighting and being dismissed in high school based on the status and power of her abuser" (Interview. June 9, 2020).

Survivors Did Not Have Meaningful Connections with Family or Friends

Based on survivor responses, the impact of trauma influences survivor progress not just psychologically but socially–impacting their ability to maintain close and meaningful relationships. Close relational ties are critical for brain development. Additionally, the intertwining of the psychological and social impacts of trauma causes survivors to define their identity based on their responses to the traumatic event rather than "typical" experiences and relationship building. Psychobiological research on trauma is inherently complex because of the likelihood that children suffering from different subtypes of neglect often have other psychobiological and psychosocial compromises and outcomes.

Within the challenge of relationship building, survivors reported being misunderstood in school and as a result enduring harsh disciplinary practices in school. Harsh disciplinary practices in school can further compromise trust between survivors and caregivers–including those in school. As a result, many girls can be misclassified as "deviant" or even referred for juvenile justice programming, or Special Education services unnecessarily. Below are the reports from survivors on how harsh disciplinary practices in school as well as broken relationships with authority impacted their success in school.

Survivors Reported Being Labeled as Deviant and Felt Misunderstood

Survivors described behaviors they can recall as a result of trauma. At the same time, they described the behaviors and tendencies as part of their development because the trauma occurred at such a young age. Survivors reported that their teachers and school leaders rarely asked questions or sought to understand the root causes of their off-task or "disrespectful" behaviors in school. Survivors discussed being labeled as deviant. Additionally, the label of "deviant" came as a result of excessive punishment in school and/or being frequently in trouble without adults seeking to understand why. Often teachers and school leaders could not understand participant behaviors in school or could not understand tendencies or preferences because of how the trauma impacted participant attitudes and behaviors.

Daisy, age 31, discussed being in the Principal's office in school often. Her parent was called frequently, but her school leader acted between anger and confusion about her behavior. "I was in the Principal's office a few times. Actually a lot of times. Before the thing (traumatic event) happened I was not in much trouble" (Interview. June 21, 2020). Additionally, Cora, age 45, described experiencing punitive consequences for actions that did not match the teacher's response at the moment. "I remember my teacher and my best friend not allowing us to go to lunch in first grade because we were talking" (Interview. June 22, 2020). Survivors who were harshly disciplined in school reported that as a result of feeling misunderstood in school they often became involved in high-risk behaviors.

Forsythia, age 23, recalled having multiple legal challenges from a child and having authorities treat her as an adult when administering consequences for her actions. "My first recall or memory was when my first arrest, before 6 or 7. First arrest was shoplifting. Three times at 18, twice at 19. At 21 it was my 6th or 7th time" (Interview. June 23, 2020). Marigold, age 33, discussed what she described as inappropriate responses to her behavior in school by school leaders. "I remember an assistant dean at the high school standing over me and lecturing me for a long time after I had been caught ...I was experiencing some ongoing trauma at that stage" (Interview. June 23, 2020)

Lilly, age 63, shared that she was tested for learning disabilities very late in her education and that school staff did not know how to support her. She stated:

> When I was in middle school, I lost a lot of time. I didn't go to school a lot and I was labeled a trouble-maker. Counselors, principals, teachers, never ever asked why. It was just punishment, suspension. Brought my mother into school but no one ever pulled me aside and asked if anything was wrong.
>
> (Interview, June 12, 2020)

Based on survivor reports of harsh disciplinary practices in school, they also recalled feeling silenced in school. Trauma is complex in nature in how it impacts survivor development as well as how survivors perceive themselves. Not only did some survivors report feeling silenced and unable to speak their minds, but many of them reported being coerced into silence and their environment being so controlled and manipulated that they did not feel safe to use their voices.

Survivors Reported Feeling Silenced in School

Participants reported similar responses around their most memorable moment being related to the idea of being silenced or being in a position of forced compliance. Anise, age 34, stated: "In 4th Grade... I was hurting more because I was being manipulated into allowing rape" (Interview. June 23, 2020). Iris, age 48, recalled being vulnerable and feeling manipulated. "My abuser liked my bus driver. She was nice. He told me that if I convinced her to date him, he would not hurt me again" (Interview. June 23, 2020). Survivors reported feeling that their voice was already taken from them, so it was that much easier for them to be coerced into unsafe situations.

Primrose, age 29, reported that there was always at least one "creepy" male teacher that she had to keep a distance from. Ultimately, whenever she felt a certain level of discomfort in school, her mom would move with her to a new city. She continued:

> There's always that weird male teacher that you thought was a creep. I knew creeps because I knew from what I went through...When the weird teachers would reach out to touch me after the bell rang. There were weird teachers in sports too. Trying to touch me, I never told on them, I just never let myself be alone with them after class.
>
> (Interview, June 15, 2020)

Unfortunately, many survivors reported feeling uncomfortable with at least one male teacher in school. This discomfort, along with the power dynamics, have caused survivors to keep quiet and keep their distance from certain male teachers.

Based on survivor reflections of how psychology and social interactions are impacted as a result of sexual trauma, academic achievement was challenging because of all of the factors survivors needed to balance internally while attempting to perform academically and externally. Below are survivor reports of their academic experiences in school and what they would have needed to lessen the academic impact of sexual trauma in school.

There is a social impact as a result of sexual trauma. According to participant responses, based on their interactions with their school systems and how their various self-identities interacted with the systems, it was apparent that sexual trauma brings to life a social impact as a result of sexual trauma. Not only is the social impact based on how individuals interact with larger systems, but also on how the intersectionalities of their self-reported identities are either upheld or dismissed in the school experience post-trauma.

Isolation, Distress, and Cognitive Development

There is a correlation between the identity marker of "experience of trauma" and feelings of isolation and loneliness as a result of the traumatic event (Foy, 2019; Offord, 2020; Vlachinos, Papagorgiou & Margariti, 2020).

There are cognitive effects of prolonged isolation. Feelings of isolation and loneliness impair brain function and cognition (Offord, 2020). Additionally, Offord (2020) reports that people that have been incarcerated and endured solitary confinement experienced cognitive impairment and malfunction. Examples included difficulty in memory, obsessive thoughts, hallucinations, psychotic symptoms, and risk for mental illness.

Most recent research by Chamberlain et al. (2006) proposes that transitional and developmental challenges for middle school girls are more pronounced for middle school girls in foster care. These girls have often already experienced sexual abuse and are at high risk for unhealthy interactions within relationships. "Cascading negative effects" can be initiated by typical middle school experiences. However, at the other extreme, girls in foster care face a number of common challenges, which include delinquency, substance abuse, mental health problems and health-risking sexual behaviors. Such high-risk behaviors are often as a result of isolation and loneliness post-trauma.

Kross et al. (2011) conducted a study to investigate similarities in the brain's response to physical pain and social rejection. The study found that 14 female participants in the study from various locations in the United States, reported being in distress. Participant brain imaging showed overlap in regions of the brain that detect pain. Findings include the statement, "people who recently experienced an unwanted break-up…think about being rejected… areas of the sensory components of physical pain become active" (2011, p. 2).

Katz (2019) provides a legal approach to trauma-informed practice for child welfare efforts. Katz discusses the isolating nature of trauma in that typically, in order to effectively control and abuse an individual, they must isolate them from their friends and family. As a result, the abuse itself often leaves the survivor feeling unable to reach out for support, which then perpetuates the cycle of isolation in abuse.

Lack of Awareness of Trauma and Retraumatization

According to the literature (SAMHSA, 2014; Zgoda et al., 2016), moments of re-traumatization are typically triggered by a loss of power, control or abuse of power on the part of the authority figure in the situation (Zgoda et al., 2016). Systems can be traumatizing when they operate in isolation, suffer from a lack of resources, have a lack of accountability and fragmentation in authority. Zgoda et al. (2016) cite public schools, federal agencies, legislative bodies, media and law enforcement as some of the most traumatizing systems. The most effective way to combat traumatizing systems is to provide autonomy to the survivor(s) of trauma as well as use a strengths-based approach for all involved.

In the United States, opportunities to learn and to utilize voice contribute to school discipline and graduation rates. Losen and Gillespie (2012) expose the rates of suspension for various racial and ethnic subgroups of students in the United States. According to Orfield, the purpose of the report is to show how offenses are addressed with disciplinary action in schools. Orfield states: "…it is critically important to keep students, especially those facing inequality in other parts of their lives, enrolled in school" (p. 4). Orfield continues by stating the fact that these rates should instill a sense of alarm among educators because they indicate a primary reason that students in marginalized groups experience distance from their school (p. 4). Orfield's suggestion in how to address this issue is that "finding solutions with professional help and training, can prevent students from taking a path toward lifelong failure" (p. 5). In summary, Losen and Gillespie found that nationally, one in six Black children, and one in thirteen Latinos were suspended from school at least once (p. 6). "Equally important is that researchers find that the frequent use of suspension brings no benefits in terms of test scores or graduation rates" (p. 8). Here, it is clear that the more time students spend out of the classroom, the less voice they have to contribute to their own needs in the classroom and in their education in general. The ultimate strategy for incorporating voice through an authentic culture of democracy is by implementing alternative strategies for discipline so that students, especially those at higher risk for dropout, can spend more instructional time in instruction so that they can have an active voice in the classroom and have ownership over their own education. Losen and Gillespie (2012) conclude with the recommendation that "… educators, families and communities work together to improve policies and practices" (p. 38).

References

Chamberlain, P., Leve, L. D., & Smith, D. K. (2006). Preventing behavior problems and health risking behaviors in. *International Journal of Behavioral Consultation and Therapy*, *2*(4), 518–530. https://doi.org/10.1037/h0101004

Finkelhor, S.D. (1978). “Sexually Victimized Children and Their Families.” Doctoral Dissertations. 1200. https://scholars.unh.edu/dissertation/1200

Foy J., Green C., & Earls M. (2019). Psychological Aspects of Child and Family Health. Mental Health Competencies for Pediatric Practice. *Pediatrics*. 144(5):e20192757. Volume 144, number 5, November 2019:e20192757.

Katz, S. (2019) Trauma-informed practice: The future of child welfare? 28 widener Commonwealth L. Rev. 51, Temple University Legal Studies Research Paper No. 2019–06.

Kross, E., Bermana, M., Mischelb, W., Smith, E., & Wagerc, T. (2011). Social Rejection Shares Somatosensory Representations with Physical Pain. *Proceedings of the National Academy of Sciences*. https://pubmed.ncbi.nlm.nih.gov/21444827/.

Losen, D. J., & Gillespie, J. (2012). *Opportunities suspended: The disparate impact of disciplinary exclusion from school*. UCLA: The Civil Rights Project/Proyecto Derechos Civiles. Retrieved from https://escholarship.org/uc/item/3g36n0c3

Morris, M. W. (2016). *Pushout: The criminalization of Black girls in schools*. The New Press.

Offord, C. (2020). What neurobiology can tell us about suicide. The Scientist. https://www.the-scientist.com/features/what-neurobiology-can-tell-us-about-suicide-66922

Sarkis, S. (2017). 11 Warning Signs of Gaslighting, Psychology Today, January 22. https://www.psychologytoday.com/us/blog/here-there-and-everywhere/201701/11-warning-signs-gaslighting.

Skiba, R. J., Artiles, A. J., Kozleski, E. B., Losen, D. J., & Harry, E. G. (2016). Risks and consequences of oversimplifying educational inequities: A response to morgan et al. (2015). *Educational Researcher*, *45*(3), 221–225. https://10.3102/0013189X16644606

Substance Abuse and Mental Health Services Administration (2014). *SAMHSA's concept of trauma and guidance for a trauma-informed approach*. HHS Publication No. (SMA)14–4884. Substance Abuse and Mental Health Services Administration.

Vlachos, I. I., Papageorgiou, C., & Margariti, M. (2020). Neurobiological Trajectories Involving Social Isolation in PTSD: A Systematic Review. *Brain sciences*, *10*(3), 173. https://doi.org/10.3390/brainsci10030173

Zgoda, K., Shelly, P., & Hitzel, S. (2016) Preventing retraumatization: A macro social work approach to trauma-informed practices and policies. The New Social Worker. Available at: https://www.socialworker.com/feature-articles/practice/preventing-retraumatization-a-macro-social-work-approach-to-trauma-informed-practices-policies/ (accessed 18 May 2022).

6 The Academic Impact of Sexual Trauma

Meet Lilac

Had there been a support group or an anonymous submission box I would have participated sooner and healed from the experience. Children don't really understand how to identify when they've been molested and how or even that it was wrong and so if educators had taught us what it was I would have opened up more to new and better ways to focus on my academics.

Academically, it was medium level rigor. I was an average student, my level of effort was aligned with how I was doing psychologically. It was a big public school and so it was easy to get lost in the shuffle. As a student I was trying to find a way to express what I was going through but my peers didn't believe me. I was afraid to tell my teachers and counselors. I didn't really focus in school nor do my best academically. I didn't really care about school. I didn't really care anymore. That's why my grades struggled. There was an indifference to it. It was like I'm here because I have to be here. Not because of homework or goals. My focus was off so I wasn't really able to pay attention in school. It was hard to concentrate on stuff. It was a challenge to do work and school. I didn't see the importance of it. Yes, definitely, socially there was a huge difference; academically I was different too. This happened for me smack dab in the middle of sophomore year I turned 16 that October. I wasn't allowed to go on car dates which is where you go on a date and the guy drives you. But after I turned 16 I could go on them. It was December of Sophomore year when it happened. I was a straight A student. After that I almost failed my first class. Physics. Its not my thing but I also didn't try. In Middle school I had an eating disorder.

Data Collected and Analyzed for Guiding Research Question Three

The data analyzed for guiding research question three seeks to understand the academic experiences for participants in the study. Based on the complexity

DOI: 10.4324/9781032648668-7

of the impact of sexual trauma, it was necessary to understand what the data showed about how participants interacted with school academically and what survivors wanted educators and schools to know about how to respond more effectively to trauma survivors.

Participants in this study reported a decline in academic progress as a result of sexual trauma. In addition, many participants reported not being able to recall their academic experiences because of the impact sexual trauma has on memory.

When asked about academic experiences in school, survivor responses were grouped into the following three categories: a) survivors reported a drastic change in their grades (usually a decrease) after the traumatic event. b) Survivors could not recall meaningful academic school experiences. c) Survivors reported an inability to remain engaged academically.

Survivors Reported a Drastic Change in Their Grades (Usually a Decrease)

Daisy, age 31, reported: "Yes! There was before trauma I was passionate, I loved to learn. I think I was even a straight A student. Then after the trauma it was Ds and Fs. There was no in between. It was a downward spiral" (Interview. June 17, 2020). Rosemary, age, shared: "Yes, definitely, socially was a huge difference academically I was different too. This happened for me smack dab in the middle of sophomore year… It was December of sophomore year when (the traumatic event) happened. I was a straight A student. After that I almost failed my first class" (Interview. June 9, 2020).

Anise, age 34, detailed her academic challenges before and after the trauma as well as her change in attention span: "Yes, before the trauma I was really a happy kid. I was attentive, I earned good grades. After the trauma, my attention span wasn't there" (Interview. June 24, 2020). Marigold, age 33, shared that her experience with sexual trauma caused her respect for authority to be compromised, which then impacted her academic progress in school. "Yes. I was in the gifted program, participated in sports and other extracurricular activities, got very good grades, and my teachers acted as if I was a future leader. My ability to succeed was assumed by the adults who worked with me at school. I didn't feel the same level of anxiety, though I had some, and was not suspicious of my peers. I wasn't angry with authority the way I was (after the abuse)." "Based on survivor reports, there is a correlation between sexual abuse, inability to connect positively with authority figures and academic engagement in school" (Interview. June 19, 2020).

Magnolia, age 56, stated:

> I was a good student in that I got good grades and was a teacher pleaser, until my grade 12 year where drinking and partying got in the way and I

> started skipping out to party or nurse a hangover. I was always the life of the party. I partied a lot. Lots of drinking to black out and sleeping around.
> (Interview, June 19, 2020)

Daisy, age 31, recalled differences in her grades and behavior before and after the trauma. "Yes! There was before trauma I was passionate, I loved to learn. I think I was even a straight A student. Then after the trauma it was Ds and Fs. There was no in between. It was a downward spiral; sometimes it fluctuated" (Interview. June 30, 2020).

Survivors Do Not Recall Meaningful Academic Experiences

A very interesting finding is that many survivors reported that their trauma was so severe and so consuming mentally that they had little to no memory of their academic experiences in school. About 50% of survivors reported experiencing loss of memory, specifically around academic experiences in school. This aspect of the study is the most pivotal in understanding how to better support female survivors of sexual trauma in school. Rosemary, age 31, recalled differences in her life before and after her traumatic event both academically and socially. "Yes, definitely, socially there was a huge difference academically. I was different too. It was December of Sophomore year when *(traumatic event)* happened. I was a straight A student. After that I almost failed my first class. Middle school I had an eating disorder…So after the assault sophomore year I slipped back into that" (Interview. June 10, 2020).

Anise, age 34, discussed differences before and after her trauma. "Yes, before the trauma I was really a happy kid. I was attentive, I earned good grades. After the trauma, my attention span wasn't there. I became talkative and school didn't matter to me. I learned how to hide behind a smile" (Interview. June 12, 2020).

When it came to academic experiences, Iris, age 46, recalled disclosing her traumatic experience to a teacher because her grades drastically changed suddenly. "I told my (teacher) in (middle school). She had called me in because I would have a semester with straight A's then the next, I would get straight F's" (Interview. June 28, 2020).

About one-third of participants reported feeling too anxious and/or lacking the attention span to focus on academics in school. Survivors were divided in approximately half with responses of either having no memory of academic experiences or recalling lacking the ability to focus on academics.

Even survivors who do not recall failing classes reported that their academic experiences were overlooked by self-preservation in an attempt to cope with the trauma as a result of sexual assault. Many survivor responses veered away from academic experiences and shifted to what their priorities were even in school when the typical priority for students was their academics.

Survivors were divided in approximately half, with responses of either having no memory of academic experiences, or recalling lacking the ability to focus on academics. Anise, age 34, stated:

> As a student I was trying to find a way to express what I was going through but my peers didn't believe me. I was afraid to tell my teachers and counselors. I didn't really focus in school nor do my best academically.
>
> (Interview, June 27, 2020)

It is clear that because of the impact that sexual trauma has on survivors psychologically, it often leads to survivors' loss of interest or ability to thrive in school academically.

Survivors Reported an Inability to Remain Engaged Academically

This category describes the responses of participants centered around their inability to engage in school academically. Many participants, because of their experience with sexual assault, reported being unable to recall, engage or maintain interest in their academics.

Anise, age 34, stated:

> As a student I was trying to express what I was going through but my peers didn't believe me. I was afraid to tell my teachers and counselors. I didn't really focus in school or do my best academically.
>
> (Interview, June 9, 2020)

Because peer relationships are significant for students during their adolescent years, academic engagement is challenging for survivors, particularly if they have experienced multiple situations of being overlooked, feeling left out, or not feeling seen in school. Daisy, age 31, stated:

> I didn't really care about school. I didn't really care anymore. That's why my grades struggled. I was indifferent to it. It was like I'm here out of obligation. I wasn't really able to pay attention in school. It was hard to concentrate on stuff. It was a challenge to do work. And school…I didn't see the importance of it.
>
> (Interview, June 8, 2020)

Additionally, the social impact of sexual trauma, based on survivor reports, makes clear the challenges of healthy relationship building with adults and peers. This challenge to maintain social connections can impact a survivor's ability to access academic material, making it challenging to remain engaged in school academically. The survivor's brain must work differently to compensate for the interruption of trauma "I felt lost. I dropped out when

I was in junior high and tried to go back a few times without successfully re-engaging. I had a lot of social anxiety" (Interview. June 8, 2020).

Cora, age 45, reported: "No one really challenged me. I shouldn't say that. A few teachers did. My mother didn't challenge me and my father wasn't around" (Interview. June 10, 2020). Achieving academic success for female survivors of sexual trauma has been challenging because of the inconsistencies around relationships, intentional interventions and general understanding of the challenges that survivors face. Many times, there is a lack of recognition of the needs of survivors in school, so their lack of academic engagement in school can go unnoticed. Lavender, age 61, recalled:

> I was an overall B student. I was relatively quiet in class. I did my assignments in school and had little homework. I skipped some classes in high school but not full days. I was never called on it. During my sophomore year, I frequently told my mom I didn't want to go to school. For one semester, I missed about a day a week.
>
> (Interview, June 17, 2020)

Daisy, age 31, stated that it was challenging for her to remain engaged in school: "I didn't really care about school. I didn't really care anymore. That's why my grades struggled. It was an indifference to it. It was like I'm here cuz I gotta be here." (Interview. June 17, 2020). While some survivors always struggled in school, many began school with high academic achievement but eventually began to decline post-trauma. Below is a discussion about what survivors reported would have helped remedy the negative psychological, social and academic impacts of sexual trauma.

Walker (2015) reviews academic literature and discusses the difference in academic achievement between black students and their white counterparts. Pieterse et al. (2010) found that there were significant differences between rates of trauma exposure between black students and white students. Because of these significant differences, black students are more likely to experience academic decline than white students (Walker, 2015). Similarly, Tinto (1993) theory states that each individual possesses pre-college characteristics that have to do with socioeconomic background and personal educational experiences, which predict whether or not they will complete and be successful in college. Jordan et al. (2014) found that not enough research has been conducted on the direct correlation between sexual assault and academic performance. Despite this, the research is clear that girls from historically marginalized communities are more likely to experience sexual trauma, in conjunction with being more likely to come from poorer families. Because of this, there is a clear need for research that examines the academic impact on girls who have experienced sexual trauma.

Low GPA, low reading levels, and high dropout rates are all associated with exposure to trauma (Ngo et al., 2008). Ziegler found that "...for the traumatized child, success in school carries more weight than for other students" (Ziegler, 2014). In addition, according to the National Child Trauma Stress Network, "Not all children exhibit noticeable signs of abuse" (NCTSN, 2003). Joyce Dorado and Vicki Zakrzewski, advocate that "It's worth noting that not all kids will act out. However, for those who do, once you recognize the trigger, kindly and compassionately reflect back to the child" (Dorado, 2013; Zakrzewski, 2013). Cole et al. (2005) emphasize the lasting impact of trauma on the learner. Cole et al. (2005) state:

> Poverty, chronic stress, domestic violence, natural disasters, and other high-risk contexts for child development may have lasting effects when they damage or impair these (three) crucial adaptive systems.
>
> (p. 43)

The Collaborative for Academic, Social, and Emotional Learning (CASEL) has established policies for socioemotional learning to help increase student success in the classroom despite their personal histories. Since 2003, CASEL has utilized evidence-based strategies to promote social and emotional growth for students in elementary and middle schools across the country. CASEL (2020) defines socioemotional learning as "the process through which all young people and adults acquire and apply the knowledge, skills, and attitudes to develop healthy identities, manage emotions and achieve personal and collective goals, feel and show empathy for others, establish and maintain supportive relationships, and make responsible and caring decisions" (p. 2).

According to CASEL (2020), there is a focus on academic curriculum at the expense of social curriculum. There is a need for socio emotional learning in order for students to grow their empathy and ability to be resilient after experiencing extenuating circumstances while in school. CASEL describes the five core competencies of socioemotional learning as self-awareness, self-management, social awareness, relationship skills, and responsible decision-making.

Blodgett and Dorado (2016) share that there is an overemphasis on Special Education referrals, which do not acknowledge the narrow focus on attempting to get students to perform academically without meeting the needs of the whole child. Additionally, schools across the United States have developed mindfulness and restorative justice as strategies to decrease "push-out" practices in schools.

Scholes et al. (2012) note that teachers voice a lack of professional development around the issue of child protection and believe such prevention programs are needed as part of pre-service and in-service training if they are to successfully help their students. First, schools must emphasize the importance of best practices and continue to standardize practices nationwide. Although programs currently exist to address sexual assault, the responsibility for children's safety is put on students instead of the adults in their lives. Obviously, teachers believe they must create a safe environment for the children they teach.

It is important that educators be trained on how to provide a supportive learning environment for students that have experienced trauma (Blodgett & Dorado, 2016; Cole et al. 2005). Very few areas in the literature specify the educational and emotional needs of girls who have survived sexual trauma. Most of the literature reports best practices in support of students who have experienced "trauma." Trauma intervention practices in schools focus mainly on approaches that are cognitive-behavioral and emphasize stress reduction. These approaches are useful because research has shown the need for behavioral therapies for survivors of trauma (Foa et al., 1991; Scheeringa et al., 2011); however, they may not be useful in helping sexual trauma survivors close learning needs that still exist and support their academic success in school. Educational leaders must be able to train educators on how to provide a supportive learning environment for students that have experienced trauma. The impact of school leadership is crucial in that all adults must learn the art of rebuilding the caregiver-child relationship (Blodgett & Dorado, 2016). Educational leaders must also be able to initiate and facilitate culture setting and community building school-wide (Morris, 2018). When a child experience trauma, they feel isolated (Kross et al. 2011; Offord, 2020), and that isolation may lead to a variety of problems long term.

CURRENT SCHOOL RESPONSES AND EXISTING PROGRAMS

The issue of sexual assault among girls in school is addressed in a variety of ways depending on school culture and the needs of the students. Many sexually traumatized girls are referred out of school and referred to residential treatment settings or juvenile justice system facilities (Blodgett & Dorado, 2016; Chafouleas et al., 2016). Typically, the number of young women living in alternative juvenile justice system facilities report having a history of experiences with sexual trauma (Skiba et al., 2016). Additionally, much of the existing research on trauma addresses trauma in general, as opposed to sexual trauma by itself (Blodgett & Dorado, 2016). Based on the literature on how trauma impacts learning (Coster & Cicchetti, 1993), it is likely that girls who have been impacted by sexual trauma will have a unique challenge in their school journey. The current literature on trauma and learning focuses on general trauma as a whole (Cole et al., 2005) rather than how sexual trauma impacts learning. Research that is specifically focused on how sexual trauma impacts learning is generally understood in the context of juvenile justice programs and not K-12 school settings (Blodgett & Dorado, 2016; Skiba et al., 2016).

Safe and Supportive Schools Grant in the state of Massachusetts trains school districts to be trauma-sensitive educators. In 2015, DESE outlined the previous grant opportunities for safe and supportive schools awarded across the state. The majority of the funding was distributed mostly to the following initiatives: Focus on Early Literacy, Massachusetts 21st century Community

Learning Centers, Academic Support Services, Adult Basic Education Services, Teen Parent Services, English Language Acquisition, School Redesign and Innovation Planning. In addition, in 2015, the state of Massachusetts awarded safe and supportive school grants (Fund code 335) to districts across the state. This portion of the grant allows for schools to coordinate supportive initiatives that align with the Behavioral Health and Public Schools (BHPS) framework (TLPI, 2005).

Mindfulness practices became popular as a result of a high number of discipline referrals in school (Martinez & Zhao, 2018) and have been utilized in schools to create a calm environment in the classroom (Shardlow, 2015) and increase instructional time for struggling students. Mindfulness is used as a strategy to assist students in self-regulation, avoiding overreactions, and increasing the ability to pay attention during school (Zelazo & Cunningham, 2007). Not enough has been studied to know if quieting the mind is possible or beneficial for survivors.

The Restorative Justice framework has been utilized by schools in response to the disproportionate numbers of students of color being referred for discipline in school (Ferlazzo, 2016) and is typically implemented to address discipline and behavior management challenges in the classroom. The focus of restorative justice is to allow the student the opportunity to understand the harm that was caused by an act or behavior and how to repair the harm. The Restorative Justice framework might benefit survivors of sexual assault.

This framework is used to address how the behavior of one student impacts the classroom community as a whole. It focuses on relationship-building while finding ways for the community to define "harm" and how they choose to address it when it occurs. The focus of restorative justice is to allow the student the opportunity to understand the harm that was caused by an act or behavior and how to repair the harm. The restorative justice framework is most effective in urban schools and schools that have a student demographic of groups that are historically marginalized. This approach for female sexual trauma survivors in school would add not just a sense of community but is created to break down harmful systems of hierarchy and bias between educators, school leaders and students.

In the literature about trauma-sensitive practices in schools, it is suggested that educators be trained on how to provide a supportive learning environment for students that have experienced trauma (Blodgett & Dorado, 2016). Trauma-sensitive practices will inform the study by allowing me to utilize participants' stories to see if their positive school experiences were as a result of their schools adopting the recognized trauma-sensitive approaches or variations of them. It will be informative to utilize the stories of positive school experiences that participants share and compare and contrast them with that the literature suggests. Some of the themes that are apparent in the literature include harsh discipline practices typically targeted at girls of color and students who have experienced trauma (Skiba et al., 2016). Participant reports in the study will be useful in determining whether or not their school experiences align with what the literature describes as a lack of knowledge on how to better address misbehaviors as a result of trauma in the inclusive classroom setting (Blodgett & Dorado, 2016; Chafouleas et al., 2016). Off-task behaviors in school such as inattentiveness, being aloof, withdrawn and disengaged, even though less obvious, are a result of trauma that may get overlooked. Not all challenging behaviors manifest one way.

Many school programs that currently exist originate from the proposal that cognitive behavioral therapies (CBTs) are the most effective when supporting survivors of trauma (Chafouleas et al., 2016). Blodgett and Dorado (2016) state that because the concept of trauma-sensitive practices in schools is new, not much is known about what works. According to the literature (Blodgett & Dorado, 2016; Chafouleas et al., 2016; Skiba et al., 2016), most efforts of supporting girls who have experienced sexual trauma are based in residential or juvenile justice systems because of the overwhelming number of sexually traumatized girls who are being served in those contexts (Skiba et al., 2016). In addition to a lack of guidance on how to support girls who have experienced sexual trauma when in school, much of the existing research on trauma emphasizes trauma in general, as opposed to sexual trauma by itself (Blodgett & Dorado, 2016).

Resilience theory, especially its application to educational settings (Toomey, Brennan, & Friesen, 2008), serves as foundational in understanding how survivors might achieve resilience in their academics and social interactions in school. This focus introduces insights into what resilience in an academic setting entails. It is important to hear the perspective of young women to understand what was necessary for them to access the curriculum in school and be able to have healthy social interactions.

Herman (1992) defines trauma as both a psychological event and a relational event. Trauma is multi-faceted because it has various effects on the survivor. Brown and Finkelhor (1992) describe warning signs that teachers can look for when working with a child that has experienced sexual trauma. Withdrawal, aggression, delinquent behavior, and sexualized behavior are common in sexual abuse survivors (Brown & Finkelhor, 1992). Yates (2004) describes psychopathology as a deviation from normative developmental processes. Childhood trauma has a negative impact on the development of the child from the time of the traumatic event to adulthood (Yates, 2004). Other symptoms of sexual trauma are described by Burgess et al. (1998) and include distrust of authority figures, aggression, hypervigilance, and seeking alliances with the most violent person in any situation are common life beliefs and patterns seen in children who have been traumatized (Burgess et al., 1998). Cook, Spinazzola and van der Kolk (2003) of The National Child Traumatic Stress Network Complex Trauma Task Force describe more diagnostic criteria for sexual trauma—lack of behavior regulation, under-controlled or over-controlled behavior patterns, and impaired cognitive functioning (Cook, Spinazzola, & van der Kolk, 2003). Grasso et al. (2014) contributed to the official diagnosis of Developmental Trauma Disorder as well. The collaborative discusses how to define and measure exposure to multiple adversities during childhood.

Herman states:

> The special challenges of dealing with childhood trauma necessitate the creation of climates or contexts that are supportive for children who have been traumatized and for the educators who teach them.
>
> (1992, p. 9)

In a survey conducted on 1699 children, 25 of them received mental health treatment services. One in three of these children were victims of sexual abuse and neglect. In addition, one in two children were found to have experienced the following types of trauma: maltreatment, loss, dependency on a caregiver with mental health illness, and domestic violence (Spinazzola et al., 2005).

The Task Force on Children Out of School (TFCOS) recognized the need for trauma-informed education in the 1960s and 1970s. The collaboration suggests that there are systems in American schools that prevent the success of a student who has a trauma history. In *The Way we Go to School: The Exclusion of Children in Boston,* the task force discusses the "emergency" that came out of the realization that children across the state of Massachusetts were excluded from access to quality care and quality education. TFCOS uses the example of how pregnant students are excluded from normal school activities. The collaborative realizes that this is detrimental to the mental health of a young woman as well as her chances of succeeding in her academics. During this time, unmarried teenage pregnancies made up about 35% of the American population (TFCOS, 1971). Psychiatrist Dr. Mary Jane England worked with expectant mothers in Boston Public Schools. In response to the question *should pregnant teens be allowed in school?* She states that "…it is important not to make changes in her situation…pregnancy may be a form of dropping out of school…and out of an intolerable situation…schools should encourage girls to stay in school and not let it be easy for them to drop out" (TFCOS, 1971, p. 31).

Existing programs that will be discussed for the purposes of this paper include NME, The Sanctuary Model, HEARTS, CLEAR, and ARC (Cole et al., 2005) and the Trauma and Learning Policy Initiative. These programs have been established across school districts in the United States—specifically districts in Massachusetts, California and Washington State, to cultivate a culture of inclusion and understanding of the problem of trauma among educators and students. However, none are established for the purpose of raising awareness of sexual trauma and raising the academic achievement of girls who have survived sexual trauma.

The Neurosequential Model of Education (NME) is a strategy developed by the Child Trauma Academy staff in which they conduct monthly phone calls to educate teachers on supporting children who have been traumatized (Perry, 2008). NME is a web-based, train-the-trainer professional development for teachers. The ultimate purpose of the program is to "guide child assessment in order to identify the primary development problems and develop a rehabilitative plan that reduces trauma behaviors and increases successful participation in developmentally appropriate educational activities" (p. 54). NME incorporates neuroscience and the development of the traumatized brain with best educational practices to form a program that is responsive to the developmental and academic needs of a traumatized child. Barfield et al. (2012) state that effective treatment must reflect and tailor to how the traumatized brain processes information.

As stated in the literature, the three states that have done the most work on trauma sensitivity in schools are Massachusetts, California and Washington (Blodgett & Dorado, 2016). Efforts that have been made by those three states, most likely are indicative of all efforts around trauma-sensitivity in schools nationwide.

The Sanctuary Model (Blodgett & Dorado, 2016; Bloom & Farragher, 2013) provides intentional learning opportunities throughout the day. It is a model that expects educators to provide a safe and supportive learning community for students and develop critical skills to reduce symptoms that result in trauma. This model is utilized in over 350 organizations (Blodgett & Dorado, 2016). The Healthy Environments and Response to Trauma in Schools (H.E.A.R.T.S.) program was established in 2009 (Bloom & Farragher, 2013) as a mental health clinician providing services to students in schools. As a result, students who returned to class continued to struggle with maintaining healthy relationships. Researchers realized that students needed more comprehensive programming and high-quality school support to address their trauma. The San Francisco Department of Public Health then collaborated with four local schools to develop trauma-informed systems in San Francisco schools that allowed students to feel safe and supported in their schools (Blodgett & Dorado, 2016; Bloom & Farragher, 2013).

Bloom and Farragher (2013) developed H.E.A.R.T.S. that is currently being utilized in the state of California and was informed by the work being done in Massachusetts at the Trauma and Learning Policy Initiative (Cole et al., 2005). HEARTS established six principles in their framework to be utilized in schools that are looking to be trauma-informed in their practice. The principles of the framework are (a) understand trauma and stress, (b) establish safety and predictability, (c) foster compassionate, dependable relationships, (d) promote resilience and socialemotional learning, (e) practice cultural humility and responsiveness, and (f) facilitate empowerment and collaboration. These principles emphasize empowerment of the child through building healthy relationship skills and promoting resilience.

Wolpow et al. (2016) wrote The Heart of Learning and Teaching as a guide for their "Compassionate Schools." In collaboration with the Washington Office of the Superintendent and the education program at Western Washington University, the team established schools across Washington that focus on support with resilience and compassion (Blodgett & Dorado, 2016; Kincaid et al., 2016). These programs are implemented by the state of Washington in an effort to create more safe and supportive schools for children who have experienced trauma. The program is based on existing resilience literature and supports teachers in empowering traumatized youth with resilience.

The Compassionate Schools initiative is not a formal curriculum, but a program that is based on the work of TLPI, and similarly uses six principles to create safe and supportive instructional practices in the classroom. The six principles are: (a) always empower, never disempower, (b) provide unconditional positive regard, (c) maintain high expectations, (d) check assumptions, (e) be a relationship coach, and (f) provide guided opportunities for helpful participation (Kincaid et al., 2016; Blodgett & Dorado, 2016). Much like the H.E.A.R.T.S. program, Compassionate schools recognize students as individuals and take a holistic approach to the child's healing and learning.

Ko and Sprague (2007) developed the Collaborative Learning for Educational Achievement and Resilience (C.L.E.A.R.) model. The C.L.E.A.R. model is made up of trauma-informed systems change in schools (Blodgett & Dorado, 2016; Ko & Sprague, 2007). This model is established for schools that are responding to students who have experienced complex trauma. C.L.E.A.R. has been implemented in thirty-two (32) schools across seventeen (17) districts in Washington and California (Blodgett & Dorado, 2016). Redford and Pritzker (2015) report the discoveries in A.C.E. studies on the link between trauma and poor health outcomes. Girls who have experienced sexual trauma are more likely to experience poor health outcomes.

Current existing literature on existing trauma-informed programs utilized in schools gives rise to my question "What does it mean to be a trauma-informed school?" Redford writes about his documentary *Paper Tigers* which seeks to answer the question (Redford & Pritzker, 2015). The programs listed above are established in an effort to begin informing practice in schools for children who have experienced trauma. A common theme in these programs is that they provide a safe and supportive learning environment as well as collaboration among all professionals in the school building. CLEAR provides complex trauma treatment as a foundation to the response to trauma within the school. What makes CLEAR effective is that its focus is on "supporting the academic and social success of students... to mitigate the long-term effects on trauma even when more formal treatment is not possible" (p. 60). Trauma expertise is incorporated into school systems and routines.

References

Aupperle, R., Melrose, A., Stein, M., & Paulus, M. (2012). Executive function and PTSD: Disengaging from trauma. *National Library of Medicine*, 62(2), 686–694. https://doi.org/10.1016/j.neuropharm.2011.02.008

Barfield, S., Gaskill, R., Dobson, C., & Perry, B. D. (2011). Neurosequential model of therapeutics in a therapeutic preschool: Implications for work with children with complex neuropsychiatric problems. *International Journal of Play Therapy*. https://doi.org/10.1037/a0025955

Blodgett, C. (2012). Adopting ACEs Screening and Assessment in Child Serving Systems.

Blodgett, C. (2014). ACEs in Head Start Children and Impact on Development.

Blodgett, C., & Dorado, J. (2016). A Selected Review of Trauma-Informed School Practice and Alignment with Educational Practice. http://ext100.wsu.edu/cafru/wpcontent/uploads/sites/65/2015/02/CLEAR-Trauma-Informed-Schools-White-Paper.pdf

Blodgett, C., & Lanigan, J. (2015). The Association between Adverse Childhood Experience and Academic Risk in *Elementary School Children*.

Bloom, S. L., & Farragher, B. (2013). *Restoring sanctuary: A new operating system for trauma-informed organizations*. Oxford University Press.

Browne A. & Finkelhor D. (1992). *Impact* https://10.1037//0033-2909.99.1.66

Burgess, A., Groth, N., Holmstrom, L., & Srgoi, S. (1998). *The sexual assault of children and adolescents*. Lexington Books.

Collaborative for Academic, Social, and Emotional Learning (CASEL). (2020). Reunite, Renew and Thrive: SEL Roadmap for Reopening School. Retrieved August 20, 2020 from https://casel.org/ reopening-with-sel/.

Chafouleas, S. M., Johnson, J. H., Overstreet, S., & Santos, N. M. (2016). Toward a blueprint for trauma-informed service delivery in schools. *School Mental Health, 8*, 144–162.

Cole, S. F., O'Brien, J. G., Gadd, M. G., Ristuccia, J., Wallace, D. L., & Gregory, M. (2005) *Helping traumatized children learn: Supportive school environments for children traumatized by family violence*. Massachusetts Advocates for Children. https://pubmed.ncbi.nlm.nih.gov/21349277/

Coster, W., & Cicchetti, D. (1993). Research on the communicative development of maltreated children: Clinical implications. *Topics in Language Disorders, 13*, 25–38.

Ferlazzo, L. (2016). Re: How to practice restorative justice in schools. [Online forum comment]. http://blogs.edweek.org/teachers/classroom_qa_with_larry_ferlazzo/2016/02/response_how_to_practice_restorative_justice_in_schools.html

Foa, E. B., Rothbaum, B. O., Riggs, D. S., & Murdock, T. B. (1991). Treatment of posttraumatic stress disorder in rape victims: A comparison between cognitive-behavioral procedures and counseling. *Journal of Consulting and Clinical Psychology, 59*(5), 715–723. https://doi.org/10.1037/0022-006X.59.5.715

Grasso, D., Greene, C., Ford, J., & Greene, S. (2014). *The Psychological Development of Girls and Women*. Routledge.

Herman, J. (1992). Complex PTSD: A syndrome in survivors of prolonged and repeated trauma. *Journal of Traumatic Stress*. *5*(3), 377–391. http://66.199.228.237/boundary/Childhood_trauma_and_PTSD/complex_PTSD.pdf

Jordan, C. E., Combs, J. L., & Smith, G. T. (2014). An exploration of sexual victimization and academic performance among college women. *Trauma, Violence & Abuse, 15*(3), 191–200. https://doi.org/10.1177/1524838014520637

Kalra, G., & Bhugra, D. (2013). Sexual violence against women: Understanding cross-cultural intersections. *Indian J Psychiatry, 55*(3), 244–249. https://doi.org/10.4103/0019-5545.117139

Kincaid, D., Dunlap, G., Kern, L., Lane, K. L., Bambara, L. M., Brown, F., & Knoster, T. P. (2016). Positive behavior support: A proposal for updating and refining the definition. *Journal of Positive Behavior Interventions*, 18, 69–73.

Ko, S., & Sprague, C. (2007). *Service System Brief: Creating Trauma-Informed Child-Serving Systems*. http://www.nctsn.org/resources/topics/creating-traumainformed-systems.

Kross, E., Bermana, M. Mischelb, W., Smith, E., & Wagerc, T. (2011). Social rejection shares somatosensory representations with physical pain. *Proceedings of the National Academy of Sciences*. https://doi.org/10.1073/pnas.1102693108

Martinez, T., & Zhao, Y. (2018). The impact of mindfulness training on middle grades Students' office discipline referrals. *RMLE Online, 41*(3), 1–8. https://10.1080/19404476.2018.1435840

Minahan, J. (2019). Trauma-informed teaching strategies. *Educational Leadership*. 77(2). http://www.ascd.org/publications/educational_leadership/oct19/vol77/num02/Trauma-Informed_Teaching_Strategies.aspx

Morris, M. W. (2018). *Pushout: the criminalization of Black girls in schools*. New York, The New Press.

Ngo, V., Langley, A., Kataoka, S. H., Nadeem, E., Escudero, P., & Stein, B. D. (2008). Providing evidence-based practice to ethnically diverse youths: Examples from the cognitive behavioral intervention for trauma in schools (CBITS) program. *Journal of the American Academy of Child and Adolescent Psychiatry, 47*(8), 858–862. https://doi.org/10.1097/CHI.0b013e3181799f19

Offord, C. (2020). What Neurobiology Can Tell Us About Suicide. *The Scientist*. https://www.the-scientist.com/features/what-neurobiology-can-tell-us-about-suicide-66922

Pieterse, A. L., Carter, R. T., Evans, S. A., & Walter, R. A. (2010). An exploratory examination of the associations among racial and ethnic discrimination, racial climate, and trauma-related symptoms in a college student population. *Journal of Counseling Psychology, 57*(3), 255–263. https://doi.org/10.1037/a0020040

Perry B., & Hambrick E. (2008). The neurosequential model of therapeutics. *Reclaim. Child. Youth* 17, 38–43.

Perry, T., Steele, C., & Hilliard, I. I. I. (2004). *Young, gifted and black: Promoting high achievement among African-American students*. Beacon Press.

Redford, J., & Pritzker, K. (2015). *Resilience : the biology of stress & the science of hope*. Ro*Co

Scholes, L., Jones, C., Stieler-Hunt, C., Rolfe, B., & Pozzebon, K. (2012). The teachers' role in child sexual abuse prevention programs: Implications for teacher education. *Australian Journal of Teacher Education, 37*(11). http://files.eric.ed.gov/fulltext/EJ999393.pdf

Skiba, R. J., Artiles, A. J., Kozleski, E. B., Losen, D. J., & Harry, E. G. (2016). Risks and consequences of oversimplifying educational inequities: A response to morgan et al. (2015). *Educational Researcher, 45*(3), 221–225. https://10.3102/0013189X16644606

Tinto, V. (1993). *Leaving college: Rethinking the causes and cures of student attrition* (2nd ed.). University of Chicago Press. https://doi.org/10.7208/chicago/9780226922461.001.0001

Scheeringa, M. S., Weems, C. F., Cohen, J. A., Amaya-Jackson, L., & Guthrie, D. (2011). Trauma-focused cognitive-behavioral therapy for posttraumatic stress disorder in three-through six year-old children: a randomized clinical trial. *Journal of child psychology and psychiatry, and allied disciplines*, *52*(8), 853–860. https://doi.org/10.1111/j.1469-7610.2010.02354.x

Shardlow, G. (2015). Integrating Mindfulness in your Classroom Curriculum. Edutopia. Retrieved November 10, 2020 from https://www.edutopia.org/blog/integrating-mindfulness-in-classroomcurriculum-giselle-shardlow.

Spinazzola, J., Ford, J., Zucker, M., van der Kolk, B., Silva, S., Smith, S., & Blaustein, M. (2005). Survey Evaluates Complex Trauma Exposure, Outcome, and Intervention Among Children and Adolescents. *Psychiatric Annals*, *35* (5), 433–439.

Substance Abuse and Mental Health Services Administration (2014). SAMHSA's concept of trauma and guidance for a trauma-informed approach. HHS Publication No. (SMA)14–4884. Substance Abuse and Mental Health Services Administration.

Walker, L. J. (2015). Trauma, environmental stressors, and the African-American college student: Research, practice, and HBCUs. Penn Center for Minority Serving Institutions, Philadelphia, PA. Retrieved from http://www2.gse.upenn.edu/cmsi/content/reports.

Wolpow, R., Johnson, M. M., Hertel, R., & Kincaid, S. O. (2016). *The Heart of Learning and Teaching: Compassion, Resiliency and Academic Success*. http://www.k12.wa.us/compassionateschools/pubdocs/TheHeartofLearningandTeaching.pdf

Zelazo, P. D., & Cunningham, W. (2007). Executive function: Mechanisms underlying emotion regulation. In J. Gross (Ed.), *Handbook of emotion regulation* (pp. 135–158). Guilford.

Ziegler, A. M. (2014). *Analysis of a Comprehensive Dental Trauma Database: An Epidemiologic Study of Traumatic Dental Injuries to the Permanent Dentition* [Master's thesis, Ohio State University]. OhioLINK Electronic Theses and Dissertations Center. http://rave.ohiolink.edu/etdc/view?acc_num=osu1405516051

7 Conclusion

Discussion, Implications, and Recommendations

The following discussion highlights implications for the key stakeholders: educators, families, and survivors as they relate to supporting sexually traumatized girls in school. Each finding from chapter four is summarized:

- Finding # 1: Survivors reported a psychological impact of sexual trauma.
- Finding # 2: Survivors reported a social impact as a result of sexual trauma.
- Finding #3: Survivors reported an academic impact of sexual trauma.

After the description, each finding is connected to its theoretical underpinnings and the current literature in the field. For each of the three findings, practical implications for educators and families of survivors are explored. Finally, recommendations for consideration are shared at the end of each of the three finding sections.

In Figure 7.1 is a visual representation of how the multi-layered experience of adverse childhood experiences may impact the quality of life of a child depending on the adverse experience. Survivors reported that based on their experiences with sexual trauma, they have learned new aspects of their identity. These new aspects intensified their vulnerabilities in school. This is especially true for survivors of color. The vulnerabilities reported by survivors often result in depression, low self-esteem, and risky sexual behavior.

In this study, participants described the psychological, social, and academic impact of sexual assault. In terms of the psychological impact of sexual trauma survivors reported feeling invisible. Of sexual assault is consistent with existing literature where participants report bearing an invisible burden of trauma (Sanchez et al., 2019). This invisible burden is exacerbated when survivors identify as BIPOC because of the history of slavery, colonization, anti-Black racism (Sanchez et al., 2019). Survivors also reported feeling unable to engage in school for various reasons.

DOI: 10.4324/9781032648668-8

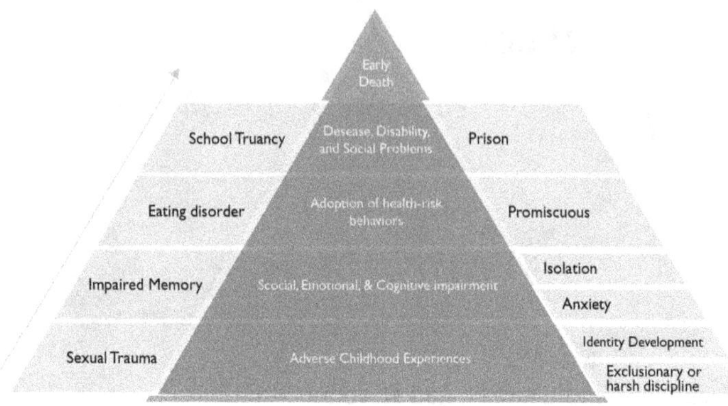

Figure 7.1 Interview alignment to ACE study pyramid

Finding # 1: Survivors Reported a Psychological Impact of Sexual Trauma

This finding reflects what I sought to understand with guiding question one: *What do sexual trauma survivors recall about their middle and high school experiences?*

Although survivors reported a variety of school experiences, all of them reported how they were psychologically impacted by their sexual trauma in school.

The most frequently heard response from survivor reports was around loneliness and isolation. Survivors reported that being noticed by teachers helped support the psychological impacts. Primrose, age 29 was detailed in her description of the positive impact that caring female adults had on her growth in school. She stated: "…they told me don't be acting like the fast girls, and talked to me like a mom. Those were my black female teachers that did that"(Interview. June 9, 2020). Similarly, Cora, age 45, recalled the positive impact that certain teachers recognizing that she was always tired had on her. "I do recall one teacher being aware that I was tired all the time. And I remember her giving me time to rest. This was during reading class. Both were really sensitive. They were caring women. They really were" (Interview. June 24, 2020).

Azalea, age 33, recalled being in need of some discussion or acknowledgment of the impact of sexual trauma in the school setting. She wondered if it would help her in her feelings of alienation or worsen them "… maybe if it was ever a topic of discussion in the classroom it would have been less alienating or maybe it would have been more…" (Interview. June 9, 2020).

Lavender, age 61, described a teacher who instinctively knew that she needed intentional relationship and connectedness. She recalled:

> I had a teacher in 4th grade who connected with me on a different level by just who she was. I don't recall anything specific, just that I felt safe with her and liked being in her class…she had a calm about her that I needed and I used her energy to help calm my being.
>
> (Interview, June 27, 2020)

Based on survivor responses, it is clear that teachers do not need to be explicit about seeing their students, but they do need to be intentional. Survivors appreciated teachers who put in the extra effort to create a safe and calming classroom environment for all students. Additionally, teacher intentionality directly impacts positive social reactions and survivor relationship building.

1.1 Connection to Literature. The complex nature of trauma based on the literature is represented in the sample for this study. Survivors reported the impact their trauma had on their psychological development as well as their understanding of their social identity. More than 90% of survivors in the study reported isolation as their primary feeling in school. When it comes to identity development, survivors reported that the less privilege they experienced, the more they recognized their social identity as being "less than" or less important in relation to their abuser and or authority figures in school.

Survivors in the study reported that their identity was impacted by their experience of sexual trauma. Many survivors even reported that their identity was shaped by their experiences with their abusers. Similarly, Boyle (2017) states that people who have experienced trauma at a young age, report a disruption in their identity. Based on the stories of survivors, it is clear that girls who have experienced trauma struggle with feelings of invisibility. The feeling of being invisible is as a result of how psychological development is impacted post-trauma (Krüger & Fletcher, 2017; Teicher et al., 2009; Van der Kolk, 2005). Survivors yearn to feel seen and heard despite their psychological and social challenges as a result of sexual trauma. The most fundamental concept that trauma work is built on is being intentional about repairing the caregiver-child relationship because most incidents of childhood trauma occur with the caregiver as the perpetrator (Blodgett & Dorado, 2016).

Developmentally, although there are differences in gender that are explicit, for example, during high school, the differences in self-perception and learning take place. In female adolescent development, more attention is given to the sexualization of young women, and this sexualization shapes self-concept (Zurbriggen et al., 2007). Kendall Tacket (1991) conducted a study that consisted of data reported by adults who were molested in their childhood. Forty (40) males and 325 females were surveyed to report the identity of the perpetrator, their age at the onset of the abuse, the types of sexual acts, and the duration of molestation. Their results indicated that girls were more likely to be molested by their stepfathers and boys by friends of the family. While many survivors in the study did not disclose specific information about their abuser, those who did share were abused by male family members. This is consistent with what the literature states about males perpetrating sexual abuse toward girls (Kilpatrick et al., 2003). For young women, having this as a context or frame of reference during development creates psychological, social, and academic challenges in school for girls who have experienced sexual trauma.

1.2 Practical Implications for Educators. Based on my findings and academic research on academic achievement, it is clear that representation matters in school (Kang et al., 2018). Particularly, girls of color need to see themselves reflected in their teachers and academics to raise achievement. Because of the intersectional nature of trauma for girls in school, survivors discussed isolation while recognizing that they did not feel seen in school. Educators and school leaders must be mindful about how schools may be perpetuating systems of oppression in school. Schools must create an intentional community that is committed to disrupting patterns of oppression (Saar et al. 2016). It is imperative that because of the psychological impact of trauma as reflected in the literature (Banks, 2006; Rothschild, 2004a, 2004b; Teicher et al., 2009), educators examine education through a developmental perspective.

1.3 Practical Implications for Families. Families must come alongside teachers, counselors and school leaders to create an intentional community around commonality of language and care for sexually traumatized girls in school. Research shows that the first relationship that is typically impacted in childhood sexual trauma is the caregiver-child relationship. Because of this, it is important that caregivers and educators become more collaborative in their work in supporting sexual trauma survivors in school.

In this study, the majority of survivor reports state that the majority of women in the sample size either do not or cannot recall differences before and after the trauma makes it clear that more needs to be done about being intentional about how families and child development specialists are collaborating and supported to support in the education of sexual trauma survivors in school.

1.4 Recommendations for School Leaders and Policymakers. This study was inspired by the hope that child survivors can be helped, and that schools can be organizations of healing. As a result, I believe, it is important to address how children who have been sexually traumatized can find support within a school environment. Based on participant responses and the existing literature, it is clear that isolation is the overwhelming feeling characteristic of being a sexual trauma survivor. At the basic level, in order for female sexual trauma survivors to feel safe and supported in school, there must be intentionality around community-building and making school a safe space. School change, when it comes to trauma-sensitivity, does not need to be expensive and complex. It simply needs to be an intentional perspective that is used to teach, lead and develop students and teachers that will organically become part of the culture of the school, which will then create a safe, equitable, and supportive learning environment. Examples of a safe, equitable, and supportive learning environment include (a) educating teachers that are committed to maintaining a joyful yet rigorous learning environment, (b) teaching a variety of histories and perspectives so that students see themselves reflected in the work they do, and (c) empowering students to take ownership for their learning. Following the completion of the study, it was clear that survivors reported multiple impacts as a result of sexual trauma. The three findings that emerged from the study were that there is a psychological impact as a result of sexual trauma, there is a social impact as a result of sexual trauma and there is an academic impact as a result of sexual trauma.

Finding # 2: Survivors Reported a Social Impact as a Result of Sexual Trauma

Guiding question two asks: *What systems, factors, and conditions, if any, do survivors recall as most supportive in middle and high school?*

All survivors discussed how their social environment either hindered or advanced their social "status" in school and their ability to build and maintain meaningful relationships in school.

Anise, age 34, discussed her favorite pastimes and the things that kept her mind off of managing her trauma in school. She stated:

> I fell in love with writing. I also fell in love with the pep rallies and other school events. ROTC was my favorite course as well. All of these took my mind off the trauma.
>
> (Interview, June 24, 2020)

Primrose, age 29, recalled that she needed:

> [learning about] sexual harassment at certain job trainings. I think once you're in middle school it would be helpful. They talk about sexEd but they don't tell people like if something is happening to you, you should tell someone.
>
> (Interview, June 23, 2020)

Lavender, age 61, would have liked to connect with other survivors in her school. While enduring the impact of sexual trauma can be an isolating experience, survivors are aware that they are not the only survivors in their school, regardless of their hesitation to disclose or connect with other potential survivors. Lavender suggested:

> Maybe some support group suggestions, maybe if my friends suggest we don't hang out with those certain people anymore or go to that house again.
>
> (Interview, June 24, 2020)

Survivors reported recognizing a clear correlation between the impact of sexual trauma and the need for healthy caregiver-child relationships. Much like the literature states, the caregiver-child relationship is impacted first as a result of trauma, which of course influences a psychological impact, making relationship building with peers and adults especially challenging for survivors of sexual trauma. Magnolia, age 56, recalled: "If someone had attempted to find out what was going on, perhaps so much trauma wouldn't have occurred, although I'm not sure that you can put a quantifier on it in that way. If I had been prompted to be able to share with a trusted adult early on in the traumatic events, maybe I would have gotten help sooner in life and learned to have healthier relationships" (Interview. June 25, 2020).

Similarly, Nerine, age 30, shared: "If I had received affirmation at home, maybe that would have helped...My dad told me he didn't like teenagers. From then on we kind of butted heads. I think that if I had had a better relationship with him, and self-esteem and hadn't dated that clown fest my sophomore year, my life would have been better and different" (Interview. June 19, 2020).

Current literature describes initiatives beginning to surface nationwide regarding programs for trauma-sensitivity in schools. Despite this fact, based on participant responses, it is clear that the need is not necessarily for overt curriculum or specialized programming but for intentionality for relationship building and awareness for explicit education around the challenges surrounding survivors of sexual trauma.

2.1 Connection to Literature. Based on the research (Offord, 2020; Foy et al., 2019; the isolating nature of trauma calls for established systems in schools that build community, are consistent and work towards a safe and supportive learning environment for female sexual trauma survivors in schools. Not only is it important for the survivor to feel comfortable in school, but it is just as important for the adults in the students' lives to create a system of triangulation (Perry et al., 2004) that will strengthen the efforts to create a safe and supportive learning environment for the survivor. Educators must be intentional about creating time to communicate with family members frequently throughout the school year to have commonalities on how to support student growth, safety and support.

According to The California Coalition Against Sexual Assault (CALCASA) it is important to recognize that when it comes to intersectionality (Crenshaw, 1989) and sexual trauma, "We do not live single issue lives." While reflecting on the work to end sexual violence it is imperative to maintain an intersectional framework on racial justice that seeks to identify ways that race should inform advocacy efforts aimed at increasing equity and equality in society. An intersectional approach recognizes how multiple identities differently impact people's lives and how solutions will recognize these complexities" (p. 9). In understanding the lived experiences of the participants in the study, their responses highlighted the fact that the various aspects of their identity are reflective of the complexity of navigating school as sexual trauma survivors. Culture informs how survivors manage abuse and how a survivor manages the abuse can inform cultural norms in their cultural subgroup (Kalra & Bhugra, 2013; NCTSN, 2008). Intersectionality theory (Crenshaw, 1989) was used to highlight the problem in this study of whether or not the stories of girls who have experienced sexual assault are considered in school.

2.2 Practical Implications for Educators. The Restorative Justice framework (Ferlazzo, 2016) has been utilized by schools lately in response to the disproportionate numbers of students of color being referred for discipline in school and is typically implemented to address discipline and behavior management challenges in the classroom. This framework is used to address how the behavior of one student impacts the classroom community as a whole. It focuses on relationship-building while finding ways for the community to define "harm" and how they choose to address it when it occurs. The focus of restorative justice is to allow the student the opportunity to understand the harm that was caused by an act or behavior and how to repair the harm. The restorative justice framework is most effective in urban schools and schools that have a student demographic of groups that are historically marginalized (Ferlazzo, 2016), particularly, those who have been historically harshly disciplined in school (Minahan, 2019; Saar et al., 2016). This approach for female sexual trauma survivors in school would add not just a sense of community but is created to break down harmful systems of hierarchy and bias between educators, school leaders and students. Because of the clear need for representation in schools among girls who have experienced sexual assault, educators must understand the impact that representation has on educational growth.

2.3 Practical Implications for Families. Caretakers of female sexual trauma survivors must move toward encouraging voice and choice with survivors. Based on the literature as well as survivor reports, many survivors feel unable to self-advocate starting from cultural expectations in their families and homes (Kang et al., 2018; SAMHSA, 2014). Allowing girls who have experienced trauma to self-advocate is imperative to their well-being and unfortunately in some cases their life. Girls in schools who are consistently being harshly disciplined are the same girls who may eventually be referred to the juvenile justice system. Referrals can create a path that can be detrimental for female sexual trauma survivors.

Girls need to feel safe in school to self-advocate without penalty. Families must advocate for a healthy expression of voice and choice in school for their girls. Hill Collins (2000) furthers this idea by proposing that subjugation of Black women causes them to be even further oppressed as they have been historically, thus making upward mobility challenging.

2.4 Recommendations for School Leaders and Policymakers. It is important to remind each other as caretakers how race, culture, socio-economic status and even size intersect to form a person's self-image. The fact that historically marginalized groups are much more likely to be sexually assaulted and harshly disciplined in school is crucial in understanding how day-to-day interactions, systems and conditions in school are or are not conducive to creating a safe and supportive environment for female survivors of sexual trauma. Creating systems of hierarchy that survivors are not allowed to challenge may be triggering for them. Any physical or social interaction that puts survivors beneath any individual or system (intentionally or unintentionally) creates distance between the survivor and the educator, school leader or caregiver. It is important to acknowledge that building trust for individuals who have experienced trauma may be challenging but not impossible. Anticipate positive outcomes while recognizing that reactions from survivors may not necessarily be personal to you but a response to what they may perceive as an unsafe or unsupportive learning environment and an imbalance of where they fit into social hierarchy in school.

Finding #3: Survivors Reported an Academic Impact of Sexual Trauma

Guiding question three asked *What do survivors of sexual trauma want educators to know?*

Most survivors reported not being able to recall or engage in academic experiences in school as a result of their sexual trauma.

Survivors in this study were able to pinpoint areas in school culture and climate where power and hierarchy are at work at their expense. Cora, age 45, recalled: "I remember in 2nd grade in a black school and struggling with reading…I remember my mom actually switched me out of that school into another school where it was predominantly white middle and upper class and that's when our school system started bussing us. In that school the teachers took more time with you and actually started learning to read in 2nd grade then went back to my old school in 3rd grade after I got what I needed from the white school" (Interview. June 15, 2020).

When it comes to behavior, many survivors saw a connection between their inability to engage in academics with negative behavior patterns. They reported needing to have caring adults in school who sought to understand before assuming that every challenging behavior needed to be escalated to earn a consequence. Lilly, age 63, shared:

> If they would've pulled me in privately. If they had acknowledged my behavior and not brushed it off as being rebellious. And if they had spoken to me personally instead of bringing my parents into it.
>
> (Interview, June 15, 2020)

Similarly, Marigold, age 33, noticed for schools not just to recognize the possible deeper meaning of challenging behaviors but to have professional mental health services that could standardize procedures for supporting survivors of sexual trauma in school. She recalled:

> I wish someone had noticed my behavior and expressed some concern at a much earlier stage. If the school had some process in place for identifying students with internalizing behaviors, that would have been very helpful. It would have been ideal to meet with a school-based mental health professional who could have normalized the experience and my subsequent feelings and changes in how I perceived my peers and authority, and who could have helped me work through that at school. I saw therapists outside of school, but they didn't help me figure out how to make school work.
>
> (Interview. June 18, 2020)

Cora, age 45, wondered why only two of her teachers recognized a need to dig deeper as to why she was always tired during school. Cora reported that she needed more recognition and training of teachers outside of their content areas so that they could better support survivors of sexual trauma in their classrooms. Cora shared: "Maybe if the teacher prodded a little more as to why I came in sleepy every day but I don't know if teachers are trained to see that. As a teacher myself I did identify two students and I did report two students that were abused. But I knew the signs. I knew the signs from watching people as a kid. I can read people but it built up an identification mechanism that I could tell something was wrong. Maybe teacher training - definitely teacher training" (Interview. June 16, 2020).

Based on survivor reports it is necessary for educators to be trained beyond their area of content expertise. Survivor lived experiences echo the need for recognition of the psychological, social and academic challenges in school for girls who have experienced sexual trauma.

When it comes to academic achievement, three of the fourteen survivors in the study dropped out of school before graduating. Based on survivor reports, this may be due to the fact that many survivors reported the abuse or traumatic event taking place in middle and high school. Many survivors also reported that once having experienced the event, their grades drastically dropped making it increasingly difficult to engage in school successfully. In contrast, survivors who experienced their trauma in elementary school or earlier seemed to exhibit the ability to successfully engage in school and reported a more supportive school environment making it less challenging to engage successfully in school. Last, a few survivors who had experienced sexual trauma before kindergarten talk about not remembering learning and being unable to recall middle and high school academic experiences.

3.1 Connection to Literature. Current existing literature about academic achievement in school among sexual trauma survivors is new. There is more research regarding how general trauma impacts student academics

(Blodgett & Dorado, 2016). Based on this, there are areas in my research that I choose to draw on research that addresses general trauma.

Survivors in the study reported challenges in being able to maintain their engagement in school. Additionally, many survivors reported contrast between their grades before the traumatic event versus post-trauma. This is aligned with what current literature states about the academic impact of trauma. Low GPA, low reading levels, and high dropout rates are all associated with exposure to trauma. Ziegler found that "for the traumatized child, success in school carries more weight than for other students" (Ziegler, 2014). Because the traumatized brain has to compensate (Banks, 2006) to be successful in school, there is greater reward when students are successful in academics at school. Similarly, there is greater disappointment when traumatized students experience academic challenges in school.

Additionally, teachers must recognize their internal biases about all students–especially those who have experienced sexual trauma. Much research has been conducted around misconceptions of behavior, attitude, posture and body language and how misconceptions shape discipline and who in the class is more harshly disciplined (Cole et al., 2005; Gresham, 2007; Martin & Smith, 2017). It is imperative that as educators begin moving toward being trauma-sensitive in their practice they begin with taking time to recognize their biases and how they may impact their classroom culture and discipline of certain students with isolating and/or off-task behaviors. Lastly, it is important to ensure that all educators continue to hold high academic and behavioral expectations for students who have experienced sexual trauma.

3.2 Practical Implications for Educators. *Teacher to School Leader.* This may be one of the most challenging relationships in this dynamic because of the unspoken power dynamic that exists and may cause either side to feel hesitant to be honest about their perspective on the work of creating a safe and supportive school environment. This recommendation would also be helpful to ground the conversation and feedback on what is most effective for female student survivors of sexual trauma. This would hopefully provide insight into the bigger picture of why the work being done to support students and sexual trauma survivors is necessary.

Teacher to Teacher. Being intentional about creating an environment of relational trust. One of the most vulnerable pieces of the work of education for teachers is the achievement of their students. If teachers can have an established space to discuss and strategize around student achievement, I believe it would create a culture of relational trust such that teachers may allow themselves to be vulnerable with each other when it comes to the work they do together with students.

3.3 Practical Implications for Families. Families should be invited to data meetings to weigh in on how to best support the student. Educators and families should examine quantitative and qualitative data of each student including data that is relevant to any I.E.P. or 504 plans. The purpose for examining this data will be to collaborate on strategies on how to raise academic achievement among this student population and address off-task and unsafe behaviors in the classroom. Epstein (2001) discusses the importance of triangulation and family engagement in school to raise student achievement. Educators should be utilized to help strategize around how to raise academic achievement in each student's classes. Based on the literature on how trauma impacts brain development, we know that language centers and communication are most impacted. There should be special attention paid to student progress in humanities classes.

Families must also keep in mind that in some instances, some of the most challenging behaviors will likely occur in the class(es) where the student feels the least successful. The collaboration of educators and family must focus on a plan to raise academic achievement keeping in mind that the student must work at their own pace, while prioritizing the need for the student to feel as successful as possible as often as possible.

3.4 Recommendations for School Leaders and Policymakers. This recommendation is inspired by Bryk (2015) five essential supports. These essential supports create a school climate and culture that is intentional about incorporating student priorities on cultural sensitivity in curricula. While it does not directly address the need for trauma-sensitivity in schools, it addresses what based on the results requires the need for female sexual trauma survivors to feel seen in school. Research shows that when underrepresented students see themselves reflected in the curriculum and the instruction they are more likely to relate, feel seen and as a result make gains in academic goals. One of the most frequent recommendations from survivor reports was "*I just want to be seen.*" on the next page in Table 7.1 is a set of strategies that uses practical skills and tools to allow for the creation of a safe and supportive learning community that also allows students to be seen within the instruction and curricula.

The framework that I have used to shape the study is the study of phenomenology and the value in qualitative research study in the lived experience. Intersectionality theory (Crenshaw, 1989) describes the challenges that women face as they navigate society with multiple facets of their identity in the midst of oppression. Trauma in its complexity causes each survivor to respond to it differently. Identity is necessary to understanding trauma because it confirms the work of intersectionality theory in that it adds value to the multi-faceted identities of survivors as well as how to navigate school given the experience of trauma.

The issue of sexual assault among girls in school is addressed in a variety of ways depending on school culture and the needs of the students. The diverse needs of students are what solidifies the enhancement of the existing intersectionality theory in that it adds an additional layer to what it means to be a sexual trauma survivor. The identity is not just the identification with sexual trauma but also how one learns–internalizes academic information,

Table 7.1 Strategies for Safe Learning Communities.

Essential Support	*Strategies*
1 Coherent Instructional Guidance System	• Establish a team of educators to contribute thoughts to revamping the (content) curriculum. Many of our lesson plans continue to contain elements that perpetuate implicit racism. This can contribute to the negative self-concept that students exhibit through negative behaviors in the classroom. • Allowing teachers that may share similar histories to students should have an active voice in curriculum development. • It is important for students to experience the curriculum from the lens of an accurate and honest history. This will not only shape their own self-concept but will contribute to their engagement in classes.
2 Professional Capacity	• Bryk (2010) states that "Schools are only as good as the quality of faculty, professional development that supports their learning" (p. 24). • There has a be a deeper level of commitment to do the work of engaging sexually traumatized girls in the classroom. • Additionally, the work has to do with understanding the full context of where students and their families are coming from. It also has to do with understanding what forces are at play against them in the real world and how to train staff to be committed to teaching them.
3 Strong Parent-community-school ties	• Make a commitment to establish a position solely focusing on parent and community engagement. • Being intentional about making culturally sensitive events at school 2–3 times a month that call for more active involvement and engagement from parents. • Having all school news, IEPs and related documentation, student progress reports, weekly behavior reports etc., translated into the student's home language to make them more accessible to parents. • Incentivizing more involvement from bicultural/multilingual teachers and staff.
4 Student-Centered Learning Climate	• This relates mostly to support number one. Bryk (2010) states that "All adults in the school community forge a climate that enables students to think of themselves as learners…this combination allows students to believe in themselves" (p. 24). • A student-centered learning climate will allow students to internalize academic habits and to create a self-concept where they associate themselves as learners rather than "trouble makers" in many cases.
5 Leadership Drives Change	• School leadership must reflect the norms and expectations they are instilling in educators. • School leaders drive change by being active in professional development of teachers and staff. However, there must first be a focus on school change that allows for school leadership to prioritize this aspect of the work.

synthesizes and interprets it. How the student lives out their academic learning is also part of their identity, which in essence adds to the concept of intersectionality as a theoretical framework.

Although the concept of trauma-sensitive practices in schools is new, not much is known about what works. For future research, it is important that schools take a look at the academic achievement of sexually traumatized girls to allow for more opportunities to research and further integrate trauma-sensitivity in schools as part of the academic discourse in the field of education.

Schools should consider investing in a paid position in school that requires accurate and specific data tracking for female survivors of sexual trauma. This will allow for conversations and collaboration between families and educators to be as data-driven as possible while providing survivors with an opportunity to provide qualitative data about their school experiences. Standardizing this practice will allow for more opportunities to conduct research specifically in the area focused on how sexual trauma impacts academic achievement and how schools can intervene.

It is important that educators be trained on how to provide a supportive learning environment for students that have experienced trauma. Very few areas in the literature specify the educational and emotional needs of sexually traumatized girls. Most of the literature reports best practices in support of students who have experienced "trauma." Trauma intervention practices in schools focus mainly on approaches that are cognitive-behavioral and emphasize stress reduction. These approaches are useful because research has shown the need for behavioral therapies for survivors of trauma; however, they may not be useful in helping sexual trauma survivors close learning gaps that still exist and support their academic success in school.

School leaders must create training and professional development for teachers in the area of supporting sexually traumatized girls in school. Teachers must be supported in doing this work and feel prepared and equipped to do so as early in the school year as possible. Research about teacher training in this area will enhance the field of education as well as provide opportunities to research teacher preparation as it relates to supporting sexually traumatized girls.

Based on this study, an opportunity for further research is to investigate the factors that contributed to the lack of recollection of the academic experiences for survivors in the study. I cannot help but wonder how the educators and school leaders of participants engaged them or if they were even engaged academically for that matter. As this and other lingering questions remain for future consideration and research, students' continue to feel isolated and struggle with impacts of sexual trauma. Having worked with diverse populations, it is a known fact that traumatized students are composed with a variety of subgroups in schools including but not limited to English Language Learners, newcomers to the United States and homeless students. Because efforts have been made to meet the rapidly growing high-needs groups in schools, it is imperative that strategies for sexually traumatized girls be part of the conversation. Schools must not only address the academic and behavioral aspects of school experiences for sexually traumatized girls, but based on the growing subgroup populations in U.S. schools, an additional layer of cultural and linguistically sensitive approaches to the work must be executed with fidelity. This will allow for more research to be done about the diverse ways that we must approach trauma-sensitivity, especially given the populations of girls that are largely impacted. The work of trauma-sensitivity in schools is not a "one size fits all" the academic and practical research available must reflect the complexity of the problem of trauma as well as the complexity of the subgroups of girls that are impacted.

The research study can be expanded and built onto the intersectionality framework by examining the exchange between intersectionality and identity through the lens of epigenetics. If considering the same participants from this study, there is potential to examine their relationship with their mothers, how the genetics formed by way of historical trauma impacted their relationship, as well as their relationships toward their children. Based on the study results, it is clear that trauma has a multifaceted impact on children. Additionally, children come from parents and based on the literature, there is a parent-caregiver impact as a result of trauma. There is an opportunity to further examine biological, emotional and psychological parent-caregiver relationships. The following bodies of research literature may be examined for future research:

- Epigenetics in black trauma survivors
- Epigenetics in black trauma survivors and their biological mothers. A comparative analysis between white mothers and mothers of color.
- The intersectional impact of race, biology, epigenetics and trauma on parenting.
- The impact of trauma on intersections of race and physiological health among women of color.

As a result of this study, there is a need to research special considerations for biological connections between parent and caregiver as the emotional and psychological considerations have been examined in this study and previous studies. In future studies, there is a need for the analysis and examination for how historical traumas can be traced as pre-determining factors to biological and physiological health as well as how that health impacts the parent-caregiver relationship.

This research is full of important learnings because of the willingness and bravery of the 15 survivors who shared their insights and memories of school. Patterns in the survivor responses show a constant interaction between the psychological, social and academic impacts of sexual trauma. This study allowed for the lived experiences of participants to be illuminated. Participant's central point of view is used to show the diversity of impact sexual trauma has on the individual. The central point of view also highlights the complexity of trauma in its nature while highlighting the challenges of the intersectional nature of survivor identity in understanding power and control post-trauma.

Hearing the voices and experiences of survivors was necessary to understand the varied school experiences of sexual trauma survivors. Understanding their positionality in their school communities was profound and a necessary foundation in understanding how to be responsive in schools around the issues of trauma and intersectionality. The three main understandings gleaned from the study are that there are psychological, social and academic impacts in school as a result of sexual trauma.

I encourage stakeholders and educational policy influencers to read and internalize this study that captures the survivor perspective to create safe and supportive environments that address the educational and socioemotional needs of sexual trauma survivors in school. The school experiences of survivors may also impact the school environment as a whole negatively or positively. It is my hope that after considering this research, that the recommended supportive school practices are implemented in support of trauma survivors gaining feelings of belonging, remaining academically engaged, and building positive relationships in school.

References

Banks, A. (2006). Relational therapy for trauma. *Journal of Psychological Trauma, 5*, 25–47. https://doi.org/10.1300/J189v05n01_03

Blodgett, C., & Dorado, J. (2016). A Selected Review of Trauma-Informed School Practice and Alignment with Educational Practice. http://ext100.wsu.edu/cafru/wpcontent/uploads/sites/65/2015/02/CLEAR-Trauma-Informed-Schools-White-Paper.pdf

Boyle, K. M. (2017). Sexual assault and identity disruption: A sociological approach to posttraumatic stress. *Society and Mental Health*, *7*(2), 69–84. https://doi.org/10.1177/2156869317699249.

Bryk, A. S. (2015). *Learning to improve how America's schools can get better at getting better*. Cambridge, MA: Harvard Education Press.

Cole, S.F., O'Brien, J. G., Gadd, M. G., Ristuccia, J., Wallace, D.L., Gregory, M. (2005). *Helping traumatized children learn: Supportive school environments for children traumatized by family violence*. Massachusetts Advocates for Children.

Crenshaw, K. (1989). "Demarginalizing the intersection of race and sex: A black feminist critique of antidiscrimination doctrine, feminist theory and antiracist politics, *University of Chicago Legal Forum, 1989*, Article 8, https://chicagounbound.uchicago.edu/uclf/vol1989/iss1/8

Epstein, JJ. (2001). *School, family, and community partnerships: Preparing educators and improving schools*. Westview Press.

Ferlazzo, L. (2016). Re: How to practice restorative justice in schools. [Online forum comment]. http://blogs.edweek.org/teachers/classroom_qa_with_larry_ferlazzo/2016/02/response_how_to_practice_restorative_justice_in_schools.html.

Foy, J., Green, C., & Earls, M. (2019). Psychological aspects of child and family health. *Mental Health Competencies for Pediatric Practice. Pediatrics, 144*(5), e20192757.

Gresham, F. M. (2007). Evolution of the response-to-intervention concept: Empirical foundations and recent developments. In S. R. Jimerson, M. K. Burns, & A. VanDerHayden (Eds.), *Handbook of response to intervention: The science and practice of assessment and intervention* (pp. 10–24). Springer.

Hill Collins, P. (2000). *Black feminist thought: Knowledge, consciousness, and the politics of empowerment* (2nd ed.). Routledge Press.

Kalra, G., & Bhugra, D. (2013). Sexual violence against women: Understanding cross-cultural intersections. *Indian J Psychiatry, 55*(3), 244–249. https://doi.org/10.4103/0019-5545.117139

Kang, S., Erbes, C., Lamberty, G., Thuras, P., Sponheim, S., Polusny, M., Moran, A., Van Voorhis, A., & Lim, K. (2018). Transcendental meditation for veterans with post-traumatic stress disorder. *Psychological Trauma: Theory, Research, Practice, and Policy, 10*(6), 675.

Kendall Tackett, K. (1991). Characteristics of abuse that influence when adults molested as children seek treatment. *Journal of Interpersonal Violence, 6*, 486–493.

Kilpatrick, D., Saunders, B., & Smith, W. (2003). *Youth victimization: Prevalence and implications*. U.S. Department of Justice Office of Justice Programs. https://www.ncjrs.gov/pdffiles1/nij/194972.pdf

Krüger, C., & Fletcher, L. (2017). Predicting a dissociative disorder from type of childhood maltreatment and abuser–abused relational tie. *Journal of Trauma & Dissociation, 18*(3), 356–372. https://doi.org/10.1080/15299732.2017.1295420

Martin, J., & Smith, J. (2017). Subjective discipline and the social control of black girls in pipeline schools. *Journal of Urban Learning, Teaching and Research*. v. 13 p. 63–72 http://files.eric.ed.gov/fulltext/EJ1149866.pdf

Minahan, J. (2019). Trauma-informed teaching strategies. *Educational Leadership*. 77(2). http://www.ascd.org/publications/educational_leadership/oct19/vol77/num02/Trauma-Informed_Teaching_Strategies.aspx

Offord, C. (2020). What Neurobiology Can Tell Us About Suicide. *The Scientist*. https://www.the-scientist.com/features/what-neurobiology-can-tell-us-about-suicide-669

Perry, T., Steele, C., & Hilliard, A. III (2004). *Young, gifted and black: Promoting high achievement among African-American students*. Beacon Press.

Rothschild, B. (2004a). Applying the brakes. *Psychotherapy Networker, 28*(1).

Rothschild, B. (2004b). Mirror mirror: Emotion in the consulting room is more contagious than we thought. *Psychotherapy Networker, 28*(5), 46–50.

Sanchez, D., Benbow, L. M., Hernández-Martínez, M., & Serrata, J. V. (2019). Invisible bruises: Theoretical and practical considerations for Black/Afro-Latina survivors of childhood sexual abuse. *Women & Therapy, 42*(3-4), 406–429. https://doi.org/10.1080/02703149.2019.1622903

Saar, M. S., Epstein, R., Rosenthal, L., & Vafa, Y. (2016) The sexual abuse to prison pipeline: The Girls' story. *Georgetown Law: Center on Poverty and Inequality*. https://nowpbc.files.wordpress.com/2013/04/2015_cop_sexual-abuse_layout_web-1.pdf

Substance Abuse and Mental Health Services Administration (2014). SAMHSA's concept of trauma and guidance for a trauma-informed approach. HHS Publication No. (SMA)14–4884. Substance Abuse and Mental Health Services Administration.

Teicher, M. H., Samson, J. A., Polcari, A., & Andersen, S. L. (2009). Length of time between onset of childhood sexual abuse and emergence of depression in a young adult sample. *Journal of Clinical Psychiatry*, *70(5)*, 684–691.

Van der Kolk, B. A. (2005). Developmental trauma disorder. *Psychiatric Annals*, *35*(5), 401–408.

Ziegler, A. M. (2014). *Analysis of a Comprehensive Dental Trauma Database: An Epidemiologic Study of Traumatic Dental Injuries to the Permanent Dentition* [Master's thesis, Ohio State University]. OhioLINK Electronic Theses and Dissertations Center. http://rave.ohiolink.edu/etdc/view?acc_num=osu1405516051

Zurbriggen, E., Collins, R., Lamb, S., Roberts, T., Tolman, D., Ward, L., & Blake, J. (2007). Reports of the APA Task Force on Sexualization of Girls. http://www.apa.org/pi/women/programs/girls/report-summary.pdf

Index

Note: – *Italicized* page references refer to figures, **bold** references refer to tables

For Product Safety Concerns and Information please contact our EU representative GPSR@taylorandfrancis.com
Taylor & Francis Verlag GmbH, Kaufingerstraße 24, 80331 München, Germany

www.ingramcontent.com/pod-product-compliance
Lightning Source LLC
Chambersburg PA
CBHW061753270326
41928CB00011B/2492